PENGUIN BOOKS — GREAT FOOD

Recipes and Lessons from a Delicious Cooking Revolution

ALICE WATERS, chef, author, and the proprietor of Chez Panisse, is an American pioneer of a culinary philosophy that maintains that cooking should be based on the finest and freshest seasonal ingredients that are produced sustainably and locally. She is a passionate advocate for a food economy that is 'good, clean, and fair'. Over the course of nearly forty years, Chez Panisse has helped create a community of scores of local farmers and ranchers whose dedication to sustainable agriculture assures the restaurant a steady supply of fresh and pure ingredients. Waters is Vice President of Slow Food International, and the author of eight books, including *The Art of Simple Food: Notes and Recipes from a Delicious Revolution*, from which this selection is taken. She is the recipient of many awards, including the French Légion d'Honneur.

Recipes and Lessons from a Delicious Cooking Revolution

ALICE WATERS

PENGUIN BOOKS

PENGUIN BOOKS

Published by the Penguin Group

Penguin Books Ltd, 80 Strand, London WC2R 0RL, England

Penguin Group (USA) Inc., 375 Hudson Street, New York, New York 10014, USA

Penguin Group (Canada), 90 Eglinton Avenue East, Suite 700, Toronto, Ontario,
Canada M4P 2Y3 (a division of Pearson Penguin Canada Inc.)

Penguin Ireland, 25 St Stephen's Green, Dublin 2, Ireland
(a division of Penguin Books Ltd)

Penguin Group (Australia), 250 Camberwell Road,
Camberwell, Victoria 3124, Australia
(a division of Pearson Australia Group Pty Ltd)

Penguin Books India Pvt Ltd, 11 Community Centre,
Panchsheel Park, New Delhi – 110 017, India

Penguin Group (NZ), 67 Apollo Drive, Rosedale, Auckland 0632, New Zealand
(a division of Pearson New Zealand Ltd)

Penguin Books (South Africa) (Pty) Ltd, 24 Sturdee Avenue,
Rosebank, Johannesburg 2196, South Africa

Penguin Books Ltd, Registered Offices: 80 Strand, London WC2R 0RL, England

www.penguin.com

The Art of Simple Food first published 2007
This extract published in Penguin Books 2011

1

Set in 10.75/13 pt Berkeley Oldstyle Book
Typeset by Jouve (UK), Milton Keynes
Printed in Great Britain by Clays Ltd, St Ives plc

Cover design based on *Ikat* pattern from a dinnerware range designed by Vera Wang for
Wedgwood, 2010. Picture research by Samantha Johnson. Lettering by Stephen Raw

ISBN: 978–0–241–95114–9

www.greenpenguin.co.uk

Contents

EAT LOCALLY AND SUSTAINABLY

Learn where your food comes from and how it is produced. Seek out a diverse variety of vegetables and fruits from small, local producers who take care of the land. Buy eggs, meat and fish from producers whose practices are organic, humane and environmentally sound.

EAT SEASONALLY

Choose food in season. Even where the growing season is short, organic gardening and farming can extend it: greens can be grown in cold frames and greenhouses, and there are always local foods that can be stored, dried and preserved for the winter months. Eating seasonally inspires your menus, gives you a sense of time and place and rewards you with the most flavourful food.

SHOP AT FARMERS' MARKETS

Farmers' markets create communities that value diversity, honesty, seasonality, locality, sustainability and beauty. Get to know the people who grow your food. Think of yourself as in partnership with the farmers, learning from them and working with them.

PLANT A GARDEN

It is deeply satisfying to eat food you have grown your-self, in your own garden or in an allotment. Even a pot of herbs on your windowsill can transform your cooking and connect you to the changing seasons, as can foraging for wild foods and harvesting fruit from farms that allow you to pick your own. Learn what the edible landscape has to offer.

CONSERVE, COMPOST AND RECYCLE

Take your own basket to the market. Reuse whatever packaging you can. Keep a compost bucket nearby when you cook to recycle kitchen scraps. The more you conserve, the less you waste, the better you feel.

COOK SIMPLY, ENGAGING ALL YOUR SENSES

Plan uncomplicated meals. Let things taste of what they are. Enjoy cooking as a sensory pleasure: touch, listen, watch, smell and, above all, taste. Taste as you go. Keep tasting and keep practising and discovering.

COOK TOGETHER

Include your family and friends, and especially children. When children grow, cook and serve food, they want to eat it. The hands-on experience of gardening and cooking teaches children the value and pleasure of good food almost effortlessly.

EAT TOGETHER

No matter how modest the meal, create a special place to sit down together and set the table with care and respect. Savour the ritual of the table. Mealtime is a time for empathy and generosity, a time to nourish and communicate.

REMEMBER, FOOD IS PRECIOUS

Good food can only come from good ingredients. Its proper price includes the cost of preserving the environment and paying fairly for the labour of the people who produce it. Food should never be taken for granted.

What to Cook?

At some point in every day, the question arises, 'What's for dinner?' That is when I try to collect my thoughts and decide what to cook. I embark on an internal dialogue that's different every time: What do I feel like having? Who else is eating? What's the weather like? How much time do I have? How much energy do I want to put into it? What's in the fridge? What's at the market? What's my budget? As you answer these questions, different solutions will suggest themselves and you'll go back and forth, weighing the alternatives. The process has a rhythm of its own, whether you're deciding on a menu for a simple family meal at home or for a gathering of friends celebrating a special occasion.

PLANNING MENUS

When planning menus, I try to think fluidly and consider the possibilities for more than one day at a time. When you cook regularly, you fall naturally into a routine of planning ahead a little. I find that the key is to shop well so that I have a good selection of ingredients on hand: some meats and poultry perhaps, a variety of vegetables, salad and fruit. After shopping, I come home and make a few preparations: season the chicken, marinate pork chops with herbs and seasoning, soak some beans. Having these things in the refrigerator, ready to cook, is a comforting start: I don't have to worry at the last minute, or at the end of a tiring day, about what I can possibly make for dinner. Instead I can consider which of those things I want to cook and what to combine with them. Usually I will begin with a primary ingredient such as a chicken. I may decide to roast it, and then I choose a vegetable or a combination of vegetables, or rice or salad and so on, mentally reviewing the contents of the refrigerator and the pantry. In the process, the ingredients I don't choose become the basis of the next night's dinner.

This process is typical for me because I like to shop without a detailed plan, feeling open to whatever looks best at the market and is particularly fresh and seasonal. I then make menus around what I find. Another approach is to plan some menu ideas and a shopping list before going to the market, and that can be a stimulating way to think through ideas and be organized and efficient. However, it is good to be able to alter the plan and the list on the spot to accommodate the discoveries at the market. If you have really good ingredients you can always make something delicious with them.

When making a simple family meal around something like a roast chicken, I tend to think in pairs of accompanying dishes that achieve a balance of flavour, colour and texture. I also consider how much time and energy are available. After settling on the main dish, I may add a salad (or not) and some fresh fruit or a fruit dessert.

Here are some sample menu ideas:

Roast Chicken and . . .

Roasted potatoes, and garden salad with garlic vinaigrette
Steamed turnips and turnip greens with basmati rice
Wilted greens with garlic, and potato and celeriac purée
Roasted winter squash with sage, and polenta
Roasted aubergine and baked tomatoes with salsa verde
Steamed cauliflower with lemon and capers, and aïoli
Green bean and cherry tomato salad
Glazed carrots and sautéed mushrooms
Asparagus with olive oil, lemon and Parmesan

To develop your menu ideas, start with a simple repertoire of your favourite dishes. Then look for other sources and recipes. Talk to your friends to find out what they're cooking. Make mental notes about what you like to eat and what sounds good. Interview those who share your table and kitchen. Use this information to slowly expand your repertoire, revisiting old favourites with different flavours or refined techniques. Capitalize on the seasons, experimenting with various ways to cook and eat the same vegetables.

Many times the best dish is the simplest: vegetables steamed or sautéed and finished with a little olive oil or butter and lemon; or a steak, a chop or a chicken seasoned with salt, freshly ground black pepper and herbs and quickly grilled, fried or roasted. These fast, easy dishes require minimal time and experience but offer maximum flavour.

Some days you may feel like spending a little more

time and energy in the kitchen, making a stew or braise, a vegetable gratin or ragout, or a fruit tart or a crumble. The stew or braise can be made in quantity for another meal later in the week, while a complex vegetable dish can be the centre of a gratifying meal that satisfies nutritionally and sensually.

Experiment with different ways to make shopping and cooking fit into your schedule. Have your family help with planning the menus. Spend a day cooking together; this can be a nice way to spend time together and cook several things to last through the week. Have friends over to cook together, sharing the work and the table and making enough so that everyone has a portion to take home.

EVERYDAY MEALS

People always ask me for ideas for everyday meals – not restaurant food or special-occasion dinners, but just regular dinners at home. ('Please, just tell me what to cook. I can't think of anything.') What makes a good meal is not how fancy it is or how difficult and complicated the preparations are, but how satisfying it is. I'm satisfied when a meal balances flavour, colour and texture, when I've enjoyed cooking it, and when it is presented with care. An all-white meal, or one that is all soft, is not nearly as agreeable as one that has a variety of colours and textures. Flavours should complement each other and meld into a whole, not rival one another for dominance. A dinner that has left me stressed after cooking is not a dinner I want to serve to my family and friends. Presenting food so that it looks appetizing and pretty makes it taste better, and it is fulfilling for both the cook and the diners. A well-set table (and this can be as humble a setting as a folded napkin and a fork) is the crowning touch to a satisfying meal, one that feeds all the senses and nourishes the body.

The following are some seasonal menu ideas. I rarely make dessert for family meals, but I love to end a meal with ripe fresh fruit.

FALL
Onion and anchovy tart
Rocket salad
Fruit: Honeydew melon

Persimmon salad
Braised chicken legs with fennel and egg noodles

Chicory salad
Braised pork shoulder and shell bean gratin
Fruit: Apples

Lentil soup and cornbread
Flan

Chopped salad
Pappardelle with Bolognese sauce
Pear sherbet

WINTER
Winter squash soup
Braised duck legs with wilted greens
Fruit: Pears

Romaine salad
Linguine with clams
Winter fruit compote

Shaved fennel salad
Fish fried in breadcrumbs with wilted spinach
Fruit: Tangerines

Curly endive salad
Boiled dinner with salsa verde
Apple tart

SPRING
Shallow-poached salmon with herb butter
Steamed asparagus and roasted new potatoes
Fruit: Strawberries

Artichoke salad
Roast leg of lamb with tapenade and steamed turnips
Fruit: Cherries

Avocado and grapefruit salad
Grilled pork chops and spring onions
with herb butter and polenta

Linguine with pesto and green beans
Baked stuffed apricots

Barbecued chicken breast
Spring vegetable ragout
Cherry pie

SUMMER
Sliced tomatoes with basil

Cold roast pork with potato salad
Fruit: Summer berries

Herb and radish salad
Summer minestrone with garlic croutons
Fruit: Nectarines

Sweetcorn soup
Barbecued fish and summer squash with salsa verde
Strawberries in red wine

Tomato croutons
Steak with herbs, roasted potatoes, and salad
Biscotti and grapes

French bean and roasted pepper salad
Baked halibut and roasted aubergine with aïoli
Fruit: Raspberries and peaches

Penne rigate with fresh tomato sauce
Garden salad
Goat cheese and figs

Cheese soufflé
Green salad
Fruit: Victoria plums

FRIENDS FOR DINNER

I love cooking and eating with friends; I think that's why
I started a restaurant. I give more thought and consider-
ation to the menu and the evening when I'm cooking for
guests, whether it is a special occasion such as a birthday
party or holiday feast or just a casual gathering of close

friends. I try to plan a menu that I think will please and is fitting to the occasion, but, equally important, one that is not too complicated and difficult to prepare. I want to enjoy myself and I want my guests to feel relaxed, knowing that things are under control.

Here are a few practices I employ to help me plan a menu, think it through and cook it. These are critical for large gatherings and complex events, but they are useful for simple dinners, too. Once you have decided on the menu, make a game plan. First write out the menu and draft a shopping list. If, when you make the shopping list, you discover that the shopping, not to mention the cooking, is too complicated, go back and revise the menu – or see if anyone can help. Shop far enough in advance that you don't arrive at home laden with shopping bags without enough time to cook – a recipe for a very frazzled cook.

From the menu and shopping list, you can devise a prep list (a list of all the different preparations that need to be done to cook and serve the meal) and a timetable. I like to deconstruct each course into its elements. Take a green salad, for example: the greens need to be washed and dried, the radishes washed and trimmed, the vinaigrette prepared, and finally, the salad dressed and served. The timetable is the plan of when to do each of those steps. The lettuces and radishes can be prepared early in the day, the vinaigrette made an hour or two ahead, the bowl that the salad will be served in selected and put aside, but the salad won't be tossed until just before serving. To calculate the timing for longer-cooking items such as a roast, count backwards from the time dinner is to be served. For example, if dinner is to be served at seven o'clock and the roast is going to take around an hour and a half to cook and a half hour to rest before serving, it should go into a preheated oven around five o'clock.

When the menu consists of several courses, it is helpful to have one or two that are ready in advance, needing only reheating or finishing with a sauce. This allows you to concentrate on the one dish that occupies your full last-minute attention. If planning allows, make something like a braise or a soup the day before, which will only need reheating and will taste better for having been made a day ahead. Depending on what it is, I like to make dessert early in the day or even the day before. For example, if dessert is to be apple tart, I make the short-crust pastry the day before or take it out of the freezer. The day of the dinner, I roll out the pastry in the afternoon and have it ready in the refrigerator. When company arrives I have one of my willing guests peel and slice the apples and arrange them on the pastry base while I do something else. The tart can go into the oven when we sit down to eat and it will be baked and still warm at dessert time. People love to join in the cooking and if you have thought through a timetable, you will know how to direct them.

Choosing the serving dishes and setting the table is part of the timetable, too. Ever since I was a little girl, I've loved setting the table, and I still do. I always get the table ready long before the guests arrive, because once I get involved with cooking I won't want to be bothered, and also because I want people to arrive and see the table ready and think, 'They were expecting me!' It also gives me a moment to imagine the meal and how it will be served. I serve just about everything family-style – the food passed around the table on platters or in big bowls or in the dishes it was cooked in. There are a few exceptions – most pasta dishes, for example – that are better dished up in the kitchen. I also like to have a little something ready to nibble on when the guests arrive. This can be as simple as a bowl of warm olives or roasted nuts. I often make croutons topped with a little tasty tidbit (see p. 34). Another of my favourite little some-things is a plate or bowl of freshly cut seasonal vegetables (carrots, fennel, radishes, celery, sweet peppers) served with nothing more than a sprinkle of salt and a squeeze of lemon. I serve this in the kitchen so the guests can mingle, nibble and come and see me while I am finishing up the last steps of the dinner.

I can't stress enough the importance of keeping the menu simple, inviting and doable. It is much better to cook something you know how to do confidently than to attempt an ambitious menu that leaves you feeling exhausted and frustrated. With good organization and planning you can have fabulous dinner parties and enjoy every moment of them.

These are a few ideas for special-occasion dinner-party menus.

FESTIVE MENUS
Halibut tartare with frisée salad
Roast leg of lamb with potato and green garlic gratin
Buttered peas
Strawberries in red wine

Garlic soup
Baked whole fish and saffron rice with
chermoula and harissa
Steamed turnips and carrots
Apricot soufflé and lemon verbena tisane

Anchovy and tapenade croutons
Grand aïoli with barbecued fish, French beans,
cauliflower, potatoes, fennel and carrots
Garden salad
Nectarine tart and mint tisane

Artichoke, fennel and Parmesan salad
Braised beef with egg noodles and gremolata
Orange sherbet and cat's-tongue cookies

Raw oysters and rye-bread toasts
Leeks vinaigrette with chopped egg
Roast pork loin with braised cabbage
Steamed potatoes
Tarte Tatin

PICNICS

A picnic is a great way to change the routine and get out-
doors to your local park, or the woods, or the beach. It's
true that appetites are sharpened and tastes are enlivened
in the open air, and the setting adds extra flavour to even
very simple picnic fare. One thing that transforms the
experience is to put the food on real dishes. Nothing too
fragile or irreplaceable, to be sure, but most plates and
bowls will survive a picnic. It makes all the difference to

see, instead of storage containers, an array of lovely bowls and plates with food nicely arranged on them and spread out on a big colourful cloth. I like to pack actual re-usable tableware (not paper or plastic): tin plates and cups, for example, which are fun and practical, or chipped and mismatched china, and small glass tumblers that are equally good for wine, water, lemonade or tea. A wide basket or two can accommodate dishes and food; they may be a bit heavy to carry, but it is so worth the extra effort. In warm weather, bring a small cooler for ice (to chill beverages and fruit and to keep aïoli cold and fresh greens from wilting). On cold days a tall thermos is handy for hot tea or soup.

Some of my favourite foods for picnics are bread and croutons; olives and radishes; cured meats such as prosciutto, salami and ham; pâté, pickles and mustard; cheese; cherry tomatoes and other raw vegetables such as carrots, fennel and celery; rocket and watercress; chicken salad, egg salad, potato salad, lentil salad, green bean and tomato salad, aïoli and vegetables; hard-cooked eggs with anchovies or devilled eggs; frittatas; cold roasted meats or chicken; tabbouleh; broad bean purée; and sandwiches of all kinds, of course. Fresh fruits, almond tarts, lemon tartlets, biscotti, cookies. Elaborate or not, plain or fancy – just about anything portable.

PACKING A LUNCH

As any parent knows, packing a school lunch that is nutritious and tasty – and one your child will eat – can be a challenge. One of my goals is to revolutionize school lunch programmes so that schoolchildren nationwide can eat healthy, delicious food that they have participated in growing, cooking and serving themselves. The best way for children to learn how to take care of themselves, how to eat well and how to sustain our natural resources is to learn where food comes from. This is a long-term effort and the subject for another book. Meanwhile, there are lunchboxes.

When my daughter was young, I realized that if I thought of the lunchbox not as the sandwich-chips-juice formula, but more like something we would eat at home at the table, I could come up with much better ideas. She loves vinaigrette (which I have found to be true of most children) and will eat almost anything dressed with it. So one thing I did for years, with many variations, was to make some vinaigrette, put it into a small container and prepare a selection of things to dip into it: romaine or cos lettuce leaves, carrot sticks or shaved carrot curls, French beans, slices of fennel, radishes, cucumbers, steamed broccoli and cauliflower florets, raw and cooked vegetables of all kinds, a little leftover chicken or fish, croutons. Many of the foods that are good for picnics are good for lunches as well. Rice salads with bits of vegetables and meat or fruit and nuts; lentil, farro and tabbouleh salads; potato, egg and vegetable salads made with oil instead of mayonnaise – these are all good choices for kids who don't like sandwiches. A small thermos is wonderful for soups or a warm stew. And instead of sweets, I would send along fresh fruit, ripe and irresistible. Delicate pears, tender berries and other fragile foods should be packed in containers so that they do not get crushed. Insulated bags offer another layer of protection and help things stay cool.

I always tried to include my daughter when I was deciding what to pack for lunch. This was not successful in the morning; getting ready for school was frantic enough already. But frequently after dinner we would take a moment to consider if there were leftovers that might be an appealing part of the next day's lunch. Preparing some part of lunch the night before makes the morning much easier and it is more likely that you will come up with a balanced combination. Another thing I would do to keep her interested in lunch was try to surprise her, to put in something unexpected. I wanted her to look forward to what she would find in her lunchbox and not assume it would be the same old thing.

Packing a lunch for work can be less expensive, healthier and tastier than buying lunch out. If you cook enough dinner and plan for leftovers, there will always be something for lunch the next day.

Four Essential Sauces

These four sauces, though basic, add so much flavour, dimension and colour to meals that I can't imagine cooking without them. Any one of them can pull a meal together and turn a simple plate of meat and vegetables into a finished dish; and they're so easy to prepare that once you've made them a few times, you'll never have to look up these recipes again. The only catch: because they're so simple, there's no hiding what these sauces are made of. You've got to start with ingredients that taste good by themselves: fruity olive oil, wine vinegar with character and flavour, lively garden herbs and good fresh butter.

VINAIGRETTE
Makes about 50ml

This is the sauce I make most often, and if it's made out of good olive oil and good wine vinegar, it's the best salad dressing I can imagine. At its simplest, vinaigrette is a mixture of vinegar and oil in a ratio of 1 part vinegar to about 3 or 4 parts oil. Start by estimating roughly how much vinaigrette you will need. This depends on what you're using it for; 50ml is more than enough for four servings of green salad, for example, but you really never need to measure out exact amounts. Start by pouring the vinegar into a bowl. Dissolve a pinch of salt in it and taste for balance. The salt has a real relationship with the vinegar. When you add just enough salt, it subdues the acid of the vinegar and brings it into a wonderful balance. Try adding salt bit by bit and tasting to see what happens. How much salt is too much? How much is too little? What tastes best? If you add too much salt, just add a touch more vinegar.

Grind in some black pepper and whisk in the oil. The vinaigrette should taste brightly balanced, neither too oily nor overly acidic. Adjust the sauce, adding more vinegar if you've added too much oil, and more salt, if it needs it.

Pour into a small bowl:
  1 tablespoon red wine vinegar
Add:
  Salt
  Freshly ground black pepper
Stir to dissolve the salt, taste, and adjust if needed. Use a fork or small whisk to beat in, a little at a time:
  3 to 4 tablespoons extra-virgin olive oil
Taste as you go and stop when it tastes right.

SALSA VERDE
Makes 150ml

Salsa verde, the classic green sauce of Italy, is a sauce of olive oil and chopped parsley flavoured with lemon zest, garlic and capers. It adds lively freshness to almost any simple dish. Flat-leaved Italian parsley is preferable, but curly parsley is good, too. Fresh parsley – the fresher the better – is the majority herb, but almost any other fresh, tender herb can enhance a salsa verde: tarragon, chervil and chives are good choices.

Use a sharp knife when you chop parsley (and other herbs). A sharp knife slices cleanly through the leaves, preserving both flavour and colour, while a dull knife mashes and bruises them.

The zest is the thin yellow outer layer of the lemon's skin; avoid grating any of the bitter white part (called the pith) beneath. The zest brightens the flavour of the sauce, so don't be shy with it; you may need more than one lemon's worth.

Don't hesitate to experiment. I make salsa verde more or less thick depending on what I am using it for. I tend to use less oil when it's for roasted meats and barbecued vegetables and more for fish.

Combine in a small bowl:
  2 tablespoons coarsely chopped parsley (leaves and thin
    stems only)
  Grated zest of 1 lemon
  1 small garlic clove, peeled and very finely chopped into a
    purée
  1 tablespoon capers, rinsed, drained and coarsely chopped
  ½ teaspoon salt
  Freshly ground black pepper to taste
  100ml olive oil
Mix well and taste for salt. Let the sauce sit for a while to develop the flavours.

MAKING MAYONNAISE

Velvety, luscious, garlicky mayonnaise – what the French call *aïoli* (pronounced *eye-oh-lee*) – is another sauce I use all the time: on sandwiches; with vegetables, both raw and cooked; with meat and fish; as the binder for chicken salad and egg salad; and as a base for sauces such as tartare sauce. Most children, even very young ones, love aïoli and will happily use it as a dip for bite after bite of bread, carrots, potatoes, and even vegetables they might otherwise refuse.

Two or three small cloves of garlic per egg yolk, pounded with a mortar and pestle, make a fairly pungent garlic mayonnaise – depending on the garlic. The strength of garlic's flavour can vary a lot, depending on freshness, season and variety. I always pound the garlic in a mortar and pestle and reserve half of it, so I can add it later if the aïoli needs it. (You can always add more garlic, but you can't subtract it.) It's important to pound the garlic to a very smooth purée so the sauce will be garlicky through and through, not just a mayonnaise with bits of garlic in it.

One egg yolk will absorb up to 225ml oil, but you can add less if you don't need that much mayonnaise. Whisk the oil in drop by drop at first, adding more as you go. It is much easier to whisk when the bowl is steadied. To help hold it still, set it on top of a coiled tea towel.

Adding a small amount of water to the egg yolk before you incorporate the oil helps prevent the sauce from separating or 'breaking.' If mayonnaise does separate, stop adding oil, but don't despair. Just crack a fresh egg, separate the yolk into a new bowl, add a little water as before, and slowly whisk in first the broken sauce and then the rest of the oil.

Make aïoli half an hour ahead of time, to give the flavours a chance to marry. As with anything made with raw eggs, if you're not going to serve mayonnaise within an hour, refrigerate it. Aïoli tastes best the day it's made.

AÏOLI (GARLIC MAYONNAISE)
Makes about 1 cup

Peel:

> *2 or 3 small garlic cloves*

Pound until smooth with a mortar and pestle, along with:

> *A pinch of salt*

Separate into a mixing bowl:

> *1 egg yolk*

Add about half the garlic and:

> *½ teaspoon water*

Mix well with a whisk. Into a measuring jug, measure about:

> *225ml olive oil*

Slowly dribble the oil into the egg yolk mixture, whisking constantly. As the egg yolk absorbs the oil, the sauce will thicken, lighten in colour, and become opaque. This will happen rather quickly. Then you can add the oil a little faster, whisking all the while.

If the sauce is thicker than you like, thin it with a few

drops of water. Taste and add more salt and garlic, as desired.

HERB BUTTER
Makes about 175g

Herb butter is softened butter that has been flavoured with herbs. It makes a great sauce for meat, fish or vegetables, providing lots of flavour for next to no effort. I like it to be really green, full of lots and lots of herbs, with just enough butter to bind them together. Poached fish served with a herb butter made with the classic *fines herbes* of French cuisine (parsley, chives, tarragon and chervil) is sublime.

Either salted or unsalted butter will do for a herb butter. Just remember to season accordingly when you start adding salt.

Lemon juice brings out the flavour of the herbs. The cayenne adds a little zing. Almost any fresh herb can be used. The more tender-leaved herbs, such as parsley, basil, chives or chervil, should be very fresh and chopped at the last minute. More pungent herbs such as sage or rosemary are tastier when they are chopped and gently heated on the stove in a little melted butter. (Allow to cool to room temperature before adding to the softened butter.) Or, with or without herbs, make a butter flavoured with one or two salt-packed anchovies (rinsed, filleted and chopped), lemon zest and black pepper, or, for an unusual twist and colour, with some chopped nasturtium flowers or hot spicy peppers.

Serve the butter as is, soft and spreadable; or put it in

a piece of cling film or greaseproof paper, roll it into a log, chill until hard, and cut it into coin-shaped pieces to put on top of hot food. Any extra herb butter can be frozen and used later.

Stir together in a small bowl, mixing well:
   100g butter, softened
   25g chopped herbs (such as parsley, chervil and chives)
   1 garlic clove, peeled and finely chopped
   Squeeze of lemon juice
   Salt and freshly ground black pepper
   A pinch of cayenne
Taste and adjust the salt and lemon as needed.

Salads

I love salad: I love to wash it, I love to eat it. As far as I am concerned, a meal without one is incomplete. The salads I crave are combinations of lettuces, vegetables and fruits prepared very simply and tossed, typically, with a lively vinaigrette. It's the immediacy that makes a salad so compelling and seductive, so use ingredients that are fresh and radiant and in season, be they lettuces, tomatoes, carrots, radishes, potatoes, persimmons, or pecans. Almost anything good can be turned into a delicious salad – even the leaves plucked off a bunch of fresh parsley, tossed with lemon juice and olive oil and a little salt.

GARDEN LETTUCE

For me, making a garden lettuce salad – washing beautiful fresh-picked lettuces and tossing them together with a scattering of herbs and a vinaigrette – is as much of a joy as eating one. I love the colourful variety of lettuces, bitter and sweet; the flavour and complexity of herbs such as chervil and chives; and the brightness of a simple vinaigrette made with red wine vinegar, olive oil and a whisper of garlic, which highlights the lettuces and herbs without overwhelming them.

For a salad to have flavour and life, you have to start

with fresh, just-picked lettuces. I'm fortunate to have a small kitchen garden where I grow various lettuces and herbs for salad, but if you don't have such a garden it can take some real dedication to find good greens. Farmers' markets are the best places to start. When my garden is not producing, or when I'm away from home, I shop for heads of lettuce and try to create my own combinations of lettuces, rocket, chicories and whatever tender herbs I can find. I generally avoid the salad mixes, especially the pre-bagged ones, which usually seem to include one or two kinds of greens that don't belong with the others. If there is a lovely mixture from a local salad grower, fine, but otherwise try to buy the best heads of lettuce you can find and make your own mix.

Wash the lettuce, gently but thoroughly, in a basin or bowl of cold water. First cull through the lettuces, pulling off and throwing into the compost bin any outer leaves that are tough, yellowed or damaged. Then cut out the stem end, separating the rest of the leaves into the water. Gently swish the leaves in the water with your open hands and lift the lettuce out of the water and into a colander. If the lettuces are very dirty, change the water and wash again.

Dry the lettuces in a salad spinner, but don't overfill it. It's much more effective to spin-dry a few small batches than one or two large ones. Empty the water from the spinner after each batch. Any water clinging to the leaves will dilute the vinaigrette, so check the leaves and spin them again if they're still a little wet. I spread out each batch of leaves in a single layer on a tea towel as I go. Then I gently roll up the towel and put it into the refrigerator until it's time to serve the salad. You can do this a few hours ahead.

When the time comes, put the lettuce into a bowl big enough to allow you to toss the salad. If you have some, add a small handful of chives or chervil, or both, either chopped quickly or snipped with scissors.

Toss everything with the vinaigrette, using just enough sauce to coat the leaves lightly, so they glisten. Beware of overdressing small, tender lettuces: they will wilt and turn soggy. I usually toss salads with my hands. (I eat salads with my hands, too.) That way I can be gentle and precise and make sure that each leaf is evenly dressed. Taste, and if needed, finish the salad with a sprinkling of salt or brighten it with a splash of vinegar or a squeeze of lemon juice. Taste again and see what you think, then toss one last time and serve the salad right away.

GARDEN LETTUCE SALAD
4 servings

Carefully wash and dry:
  4 generous handfuls of lettuce
Mix together:
  1 garlic clove, peeled and pounded to a fine purée
  1 tablespoon red wine vinegar
  Salt
  Freshly ground black pepper
Stir to dissolve the salt, taste, and adjust if needed. Whisk in:
  3 to 4 tablespoons olive oil
Use a lettuce leaf to taste the vinaigrette as you add the

27

oil. Put the lettuce into a large bowl, add about three quarters of the vinaigrette, toss and taste. Add more dressing as needed. Serve immediately.

Variations

Lettuces vary in availability according to season. Romaine or cos lettuce is usually best in the summertime. Fall and winter bring heartier lettuces such as the chicories (radicchio, escarole, Belgian endive and frisée or curly endive).

PUTTING A SALAD TOGETHER

A salad of many ingredients, either all tossed together or dressed separately and arranged on a plate, is called a 'composed' salad. A composed salad such as the Greek salad that follows is a hearty dish; with some crusty bread, it could be the main event of a dinner on a warm night. Or, a composed salad might be a delicate arrangement of, say, a few pieces of crabmeat, some grapefruit segments, and a little curly endive in a creamy dressing, served as an elegant first course. Almost anything can be an element in a composed salad: all the various lettuces and salad greens, of course, but also raw or cooked vegetables, chopped, diced or cut into thin shavings; roasted meats cut into cubes or thin slices; tuna and other fish or shellfish; and hard-cooked eggs, quartered or chopped.

Tasty leftovers can be delicious in a composed salad. Don't combine too many ingredients into a single salad or it will have too many conflicting flavours. The components should be chosen thoughtfully with regard to the tastes and textures they contribute, and the dressing must complement them all. Sometimes a vinaigrette works best, when a tangy sauce is needed; sometimes mayonnaise, for mellow richness; at other times, a creamy sauce. A potato salad, for example, can be made with any of these dressings, and each will yield a distinctly different salad.

When dressing a composed salad that includes both tender lettuces and heavier ingredients such as artichoke hearts or pieces of fruit, dress all the heavier elements separately and arrange them around the tossed lettuces on a platter. Otherwise the salad is hard to serve because everything ends up at the bottom and the leaves get crushed. Even salads that have no lettuce should be assembled carefully. What's most important is that each ingredient be tasty on its own. Taste everything and season each element with a little salt or dressing as needed before adding it to the whole. When things are tossed together, don't overmix, or the parts will start to lose their distinctiveness, muddying the flavours and spoiling the look of the salad. (You can always arrange a salad and drizzle vinaigrette over it, or even pass the vinaigrette in a jug.)

As for what to include in such a salad and how to dress it, taste each ingredient before you decide. That is really the only rule you must follow, and while it may sound frustratingly vague, as you acquire a little salad-making experience, you'll begin to recognize and remember the flavours you like and the ones that you like together.

GREEK SALAD
4 servings

Cut out the stem end and cut into wedges:
>   *2 small ripe tomatoes*

Season with:
>   *Salt*

Peel, cut in half lengthwise and thickly slice:
>   *1 medium cucumber*

(If the seeds are large, remove them by scraping a spoon down the centre of the halved cucumber.)

Peel and thinly slice:
>   *½ small red onion or 5 spring onions*

Cut in half, core and seed and slice thinly:
>   *1 small sweet red pepper*

Rinse (and if you prefer, pit):
>   *About 40g black olives (2 or 3 olives per person)*

Break up or cut into small pieces:
>   *100g feta cheese*

Make a vinaigrette. Mix:
>   *2 teaspoons red wine vinegar*
>   *1 teaspoon lemon juice (optional)*
>   *2 teaspoons chopped, fresh oregano*
>   *Salt and freshly ground black pepper*

Whisk in:
>   *6 tablespoons extra-virgin olive oil*

Season the cucumber and onions with salt. Taste the tomatoes and season again if they need it. Gently toss the vegetables with about three quarters of the vinaigrette. Taste and add more salt or vinegar as needed. The salad can sit for a few minutes to let the flavours blend together. Just before serving, gently toss the salad again and garnish with the cheese and olives. Spoon over the remaining vinaigrette.

Variations

Serve the salad over a few leaves of romaine or other lettuce. A few salt-packed anchovies, rinsed and filleted, make a nice garnish. Dried oregano may be substituted for fresh, but use only 1 teaspoon.

MAKING SALADS FROM FRUIT

I wanted to be sure to include a few words about fruit salads – not sweet fruit cocktails in heavy syrup, but savoury salads made like other composed salads. These may consist of fresh fruit alone, or fresh fruit combined with lettuces or other salad greens, with nuts and cheese often added for richness and texture. When there are no greens available and I desperately want something fresh, fruit salads are refreshing alternatives, either at the beginning or the end of a meal. Figs, apples, pears, pomegranates, persimmons and almost all of the citrus fruits make good salads, with or without greens. All these fruits of fall and winter have an affinity for hearty chicories such as escarole, radicchio and curly endive. Among my favourite fruit salads are an orange salad with black olives; avocado slices and grapefruit segments; persimmons or Chinese pears with nuts and balsamic vinegar; and orange slices with marinated beetroot.

Oranges and other citrus fruits need to be peeled and segmented for a salad. When peeling the fruit, you want to remove all the outer peel and the membranes that enclose the segments, exposing the juicy fruit inside. You will need a small, sharp knife to do this. First, slice off the top and bottom of each fruit, slicing deeply enough to expose the inner flesh. Then, position your knife blade at the top where the fruit and peel meet, and carefully cut down following the contours of the fruit. Continue around the fruit, cutting from top to bottom, rotating the orange, until all the peel and membrane are removed. Trim away any remaining white bits of membrane. You can then slice the orange crosswise or cut between the membranes to free the individual segments.

Apples and pears can be peeled or not, but to avoid oxidation, which turns the cut surfaces brown, they should be prepared just before serving. Persimmons must be peeled; this can be done in advance, but keep them covered so they don't dry out.

Fruit salads are usually dressed very simply, sometimes with nothing more than a drizzle of olive oil or vinegar, or with a vinaigrette made of some citrus juice and a touch of vinegar, a little chopped shallot, salt, pepper and olive oil.

ORANGE AND OLIVE SALAD
4 servings

Remove the peel and membrane, exposing the juicy flesh, of:

4 small or 3 medium oranges

Slice into 5-mm-thick round pinwheels and arrange them on a plate.

Cut in half lengthwise, peel and slice thinly:

   1 small red onion

Onion slices cut horizontally are prettier than slices cut lengthwise. If the onions are particularly strong, soak them in ice water for 5 to 10 minutes. Drain them well before adding to the salad.

Make a vinaigrette. Mix together:

   2 tablespoons orange juice

   1 teaspoon red wine vinegar

   Salt and freshly ground black pepper

Whisk in:

   2 tablespoons olive oil

Taste and adjust with more salt and vinegar as needed. Scatter the onion slices over the oranges and spoon the vinaigrette over.

Garnish with:

   Small black olives (4 or 5 per person)

I prefer to serve the olives unpitted to preserve their integrity and beauty, but be sure to tell your friends so they know the pits are there. Use niçoise olives if you can find them, but any briny black olives will do (large ones can be coarsely chopped, if you like).

Bread

There is something magical about mixing flour, yeast, salt and water together and having it turn into a loaf of bread. Although I am not a baker and have a wonderful bakery in my neighbourhood, I sometimes bake bread or pizza at home for the sheer pleasure of handling the dough, seeing it rise and smelling the irresistible warm yeasty aroma that fills the whole house. Furthermore, *everyone* loves homemade bread: I've never seen a homemade loaf of bread linger uneaten, even an imperfect one that didn't rise high enough or that baked a little too long or not quite long enough.

CROUTONS

For a quick bite to eat, or when a few guests are about to arrive and I want to have a little something ready, a crouton is the first thing I think of. Croutons, croutes, crostini, toast and bruschetta are all names for variously sized pieces of bread, usually toasted or grilled, sometimes dried out in the oven, sometimes fried. A bruschetta is a thick piece of bread that is chargrilled over an open fire, or toasted, and rubbed with garlic and drizzled with olive oil, to be served either as is or piled high with juicy tomatoes and basil. Croutons, crostini and toasts usually refer to thin slices of bread, but croutons can also be small pieces of bread cut into cubes or torn into irregular pieces and either toasted or fried in butter or olive oil and used to garnish a soup or a salad.

Any good-quality bread will make a good crouton. A thick slice of a big round, country-style loaf grilled and drizzled with extra-virgin olive oil makes a distinctly different crouton from a thin triangular toasted slice of dense white bread with its crusts cut off, brushed with melted butter, and one point dipped in chopped parsley before serving. The croutons I make most often are sliced from a big round loaf of sourdough bread. They're usually not uniform sizes and I always oil them *after* toasting, just after I've rubbed some garlic on them.

Roughly torn pieces of bread (what's sometimes called pulled bread), toasted in the oven and tossed in oil, make good croutons for a salad.

Baguettes are handy for croutons because they can be easily sliced into regular rounds or cut on the diagonal into long ovals, which are good for dipping into broad bean purée or tapenade.

For croutons that are more evenly browned and crunchier and that have a more fried taste, oil or butter the bread slices before you cook them. Small croutons can be tossed in a bowl with oil or melted butter before going into the oven. Place larger, flat croutons in a single layer on a baking sheet, brush with oil or butter, and bake in a preheated 180°C/350°F/gas 4 oven until they just start to turn golden at the edges. Keep an eye on them; the timing will vary greatly, depending on the kind of bread used, how dry it is and how thick it's cut. For a tasty garnish to a soup or salad, toss croutons hot out of the oven with chopped garlic and herbs.

Fry little cubed croutons in butter to strew atop a delicate puréed soup. Use enough butter to coat the pan generously, adding more as it is absorbed by the croutons, stirring or tossing frequently over medium heat until the croutons are golden brown.

To chargrill slices of bread, place them on the grill rack over a bed of medium-hot coals for a minute or two on each side. The bread should have nice charred marks from the grill and be golden brown here and there. I rub the slices with a clove of garlic and drizzle olive oil over the bread after it's grilled.

Croutons taste best when they are made fresh, but the bread can be cut in advance. Wrap the bread slices in a kitchen towel to keep them from drying out (croutons tend to warp and curl up if left uncovered). When ready to serve, the bread can be quickly laid out and toasted.

MAKING BREAD

When it comes to making bread, many things affect the outcome, some more obvious than others. Most important is the flour. You cannot make good bread from mediocre flour. Choose flour that is unbleached, untreated and free of additives. All flours, and especially wholegrain flours, will eventually spoil and taste and smell rancid. Try to buy flour that's relatively fresh; your best bet is to look for a local organic-food retailer with a rapid turnover who sells in bulk.

The water makes a difference, too; both its temperature and its quantity influence texture. The type of leavening agent and the length of time bread is allowed to sit and rise will both affect the outcome enormously: quickbreads made with bicarbonate of soda or baking powder are tender and almost cakelike, while breads leavened with fresh yeast and given repeated slow risings will be the chewiest and crustiest, with the most complex flavours. Weather also affects bread: humidity, heat and cold each exerts its own influence. All this makes baking ever-changing and forever fascinating.

There is a world of breads: quickbreads such as cornbread and Irish soda bread that are easy to put on the table at relatively short notice; wonderful flatbreads such as tortillas fresh off the griddle or whole-wheat-flour puris that puff up when they're fried or pita bread grilled over a fire; the classic yeasted breads of France and Italy and my everyday favourite, naturally leavened bread or sourdough. This is leavened with a natural starter of fresh yeast and allowed a long, slow fermentation and rising period in canvas-lined baskets. Traditionally, before each batch is baked, some of the starter is held back to leaven the next batch. Rather than give a recipe for a naturally levained-type bread (which is a little complicated), I offer here a recipe for a dough that's versatile enough to be formed and baked as a flat crusty focaccia or a traditional pizza. (Kids love to stretch out the dough and make their own pizzas.)

HERB BREAD OR PIZZA DOUGH
Makes one focaccia or two 25-cm pizzas

Stir together:
> 2 teaspoons dry yeast
> 100 ml lukewarm water

Add and mix well:
> 25g unbleached plain white flour
> 25g rye flour

Allow this mixture to sit until quite bubbly, about 30 minutes. Mix together in another bowl:
> 325g unbleached plain white flour
> 1 teaspoon salt

Stir this into the yeast and flour mixture with:
> 175ml cold water
> 50ml olive oil

Mix thoroughly by hand or in an electric stand mixer. If working by hand, turn the dough out on to a lightly floured board and knead until the dough is soft and elastic, about 5 minutes. If the dough is too wet and sticky, add more flour, but only enough to form a soft, slightly sticky dough. Or use the mixer, fitted with the dough hook, and knead for about 5 minutes. The dough is the right texture when it pulls away from the sides of the bowl of the mixer, but still adheres to the bottom. A very soft, slightly moist dough will make the best focaccia.

Put the dough into a large bowl, cover and let rise in a warm place until doubled in size, about 2 hours. For an even better-tasting and more supple dough, let the dough rise slowly overnight in the refrigerator. (Remove from the refrigerator 2 hours before shaping.)

Generously oil a 25- by 38.5-cm rimmed baking tray or sheet. Gently remove the dough from the bowl and flatten it on the baking tray, shaping it to fit by gently pressing down from the centre out towards the edges. If the dough starts to resist and spring back, let it rest for 10 minutes, then continue shaping. Try not to deflate or smash all of the air out of the dough as you are shaping it. Dimple the surface of the dough by lightly poking it with your fingertips. Drizzle with:

2 tablespoons olive oil

Cover and let rise until doubled in height, about 2 hours.

While the dough is rising, preheat the oven to 230°C/450°F/gas 8. If you have one, place a baking stone on the lower rack and let it heat for 30 minutes before baking the bread. Sprinkle the dough with:

1 teaspoon coarse sea salt

and put the baking tray directly on the stone. Bake the focaccia until golden and crisp on the top and bottom, about 20 to 25 minutes. Invert the tray to remove the bread and place on a rack to cool.

MAKING PIZZA

To make pizzas, instead of shaping the dough into a rectangle, divide the dough in two and form each piece into a nice, smooth ball. Allow the dough balls to rest at room temperature, wrapped loosely in polythene, for an hour or so. Flatten each ball into a disc about 12.5 or 15cm in diameter, flour lightly, cover and let rest for another 15 minutes. Place a baking stone on the lowest rack in the oven (remove the other racks for easy access). Preheat the oven to its highest setting.

Gently stretch one of the discs into a round roughly 25cm in diameter and put on to a floured peel or an inverted baking sheet. Brush the dough with olive oil and, leaving a 1-cm border uncovered, top with your choice of ingredients such as chopped garlic, fresh tomato sauce and mozzarella cheese; long-cooked onions, herbs and anchovies; sautéed greens and sausage; and on and on. Slide the pizza on to the baking stone and bake until the crust is browned, about 10 minutes.

Stock and Soup

When I first started cooking, I never liked soup – because I didn't know how to make it! I was naïve; I thought the process was nothing more than putting leftovers in a pot, heating them with stock or water and – *voilà!* Soup. Eventually I realized that it's necessary to learn some simple techniques for maximizing flavour: how to make a good stock; how to begin a soup with a base of softened vegetables and herbs; and how to add either a single vegetable, for a pure and simple soup, or a combination of many vegetables (as well as pasta, meat or fish), for a more complicated one. The variations are endless.

MAKING A STOCK

The basis of many soups is a stock of meat and vegetables (or vegetables alone), which provides a foundation of body and flavour. A sufficiently rich and fragrant stock makes a wonderful soup all by itself. I love a bowl of chicken stock garnished with a bit of pasta and parsley or a poached egg. Stock is not only easy to make, it's one of the few things I freeze so as to have the makings of a soup or a risotto always at hand.

I use a whole chicken to make stock, which may seem extravagant, but it produces lots of sweet, fragrant and full-bodied stock. (After an hour of cooking you can lift the chicken out of the pot, remove the breasts and then return the rest to the pot. The poached breasts make a great meal, especially with a little salsa verde.) It is the meat that makes the difference to the stock. If you use bones, choose meaty ones, such as necks, backs and wings. Meatless bones yield a thin stock. The leftover carcass of a roast chicken can also be added to the stock. The roasted meat adds depth of flavour. (Leftover barbecued chicken bones are not recommended; they make an acrid, smoky-tasting stock.)

When making stock from a whole chicken, include the neck from inside the cavity. Also, remove and unwrap the giblets (usually the heart, gizzard and liver). Put the gizzard and heart into the stock, but save the liver for some other purpose. Always start the stock with cold water; the flavour is drawn out of the meat and bones as it heats up to the boil. The amount of water you use will determine the intensity of your stock. A chicken barely submerged in water will produce a very rich, fragrant soup. Adding more water will make a lighter, more delicate stock.

Bring the stock to a full rolling boil and then turn it down right away. The boil causes all the blood and extra proteins to coagulate into a foam that rises and collects at the top where you can skim it off, ensuring a clearer stock. If the stock is allowed to boil for long it will turn cloudy and the fat may emulsify, bonding with the water and making the stock murky and greasy.

When skimming the stock, use a ladle and remove only the foam, not the fat. The fat contributes lots of flavour as the stock cooks and it can all be removed at the end. Add the vegetables after you have skimmed off the foam; that way they don't get in the way. Add the vegetables either whole or in large pieces so they don't fall apart and cloud the stock.

Salt helps develop the flavour as the stock cooks and makes a much more flavourful stock than if you were to · add all the salt at the end. Don't add too much, though. The stock will lose volume to evaporation as it cooks, so it should start out under-seasoned.

Cook the stock at a simmer, which means at a very gentle boil with bubbles just breaking the surface of the liquid at irregular intervals. If by accident the stock is cooking too quickly and has reduced, add some more water and return to a simmer.

Stock should cook long enough to extract all the flavour from the meat and bones, but not so long that it starts to lose its delicacy and freshness. For chicken stock allow 4 to 5 hours. Taste the stock often as it cooks and turn off the heat when it is full of flavour. When you taste, spoon out a little and salt it to get a better idea of how it will taste when it is fully seasoned. Try this at different times throughout the cooking process to discover how the flavours develop.

Strain the stock when it has finished cooking. Ladle it out of the pot and pass it through a strainer into a non-reactive container. For a very clear stock, strain it again through a clean wet cotton towel or cheesecloth.

If you plan to use the stock right away, skim off the fat. I only do this if I am using the stock right away. Otherwise, allow the stock to cool and refrigerate it with its fat, which solidifies on top, helping to preserve the stock and its flavour. The cold, hard fat is easy to lift off. Do not cover the stock until it's cool or it may not cool down fast enough in the refrigerator and will ferment and turn sour. (This has happened to me. You will know right away that it has spoiled.) The stock will keep for one week in the refrigerator or for three months in the freezer. It's handy to freeze the stock in 1- or 2-litre containers so you won't have to thaw out more than you'll need. It is always safest to bring refrigerated or frozen stock back to a full boil before using.

CHICKEN STOCK
Makes about 5 litres

Put into a large pot:
> *1 whole chicken, 1.5 to 1.8kg*

Pour in:
> *5 litres cold water*

Place over high heat, bring to the boil, then turn the heat to low. Skim the stock. Add:
> *1 carrot, peeled*
> *1 onion, peeled and halved*
> *1 head of garlic, cut in half*
> *1 celery stalk*
> *Salt*
> *½ teaspoon black peppercorns*
> *1 herb bouquet of parsley and thyme sprigs and a large*
> *bay leaf*

Simmer the stock for about 4 to 5 hours. Strain. If using immediately, skim off the fat and season with salt to taste. Serve hot, or allow to cool and then refrigerate or freeze.

A SIMPLE VEGETABLE SOUP

The simple soup I make most often starts with a base of softened onions to which one or two vegetables are added. The soup is moistened with stock or water and simmered until the vegetables are tender.

First, onions are gently cooked in butter or oil until soft and flavourful. A heavy-bottomed pot makes all the difference for this: it disperses the heat evenly, making it easier to cook vegetables slowly without browning. The amount of fat is important, too. You want enough butter or oil to really coat the onions. After 15 minutes or so of slow cooking, the onions will be transformed into a very soft, translucent, sweet base for the soup.

Next, add a vegetable, such as carrots, sliced uniformly for even cooking. (Otherwise you will have underdone and overdone vegetables in your soup.) Salt generously (enough for the vegetables to taste good on their own) and continue cooking for a few minutes. This preliminary sea-soning and cooking infuses the fat with the perfume and flavour of the vegetables. (The fat disperses the flavour throughout the soup.) This is an important technique, not just for soup but for cooking in general: building and developing flavour at each step before moving on.

Now add stock or water, bring to the boil, and reduce to a simmer. Cook until the vegetables are tender but not falling apart. The soup will not taste finished until the vegetables have cooked through and given their flavour to the stock. Keep tasting. It is wonderful to discover how the flavours change and develop as the soup cooks. Does it need more salt? If you're unsure, season a small spoonful and see if it tastes better with more. This is the only way you can find out.

Many, many vegetables will make great soup when you follow this formula. The only variable is the length of time they take to cook. The best way to keep track is to keep tasting as you go. Some favourite vegetable soups that jump to mind are: turnip and turnip greens, sweetcorn, potato and leek, butternut squash and onion.

A vegetable soup made this way, with a flavourful stock rather than water, and served as a rustic, 'brothy' soup, will be delicious. (In fact, if the stock is rich enough, I sometimes skip any precooking in butter and add both onions and vegetables directly to the simmering stock.) If the soup is made with water instead of stock, and puréed to a uniform texture, the result will be a more delicate soup dominated by the pure flavour of the vegetables themselves. This is especially desirable for soups made from sweet, tender vegetables such as broad beans, peas or sweetcorn. I purée such soups through a food mill, but you can also use a blender, which generates finer purées. Do be careful when using a blender to purée hot soup: always make sure the lid has an open vent hole to let the steam escape so that the whole lot doesn't explode.

Various garnishes and enrichments can be added when you serve the soup. Many cooks finish a puréed soup by spooning in a dollop of cream or stirring in a lump of butter, and a last-minute addition of herbs and spices or a squeeze of lemon can be enlivening. But use discretion; a garnish can overcomplicate or overpower the flavour of the soup itself.

CARROT SOUP
8 servings

Melt in a heavy-bottomed pot:
   50g butter
Add:
   2 onions, sliced
   1 thyme sprig
Cook over medium-low heat until tender, about 10 minutes. Add:
   1kg carrots, peeled and sliced
Season with:
   Salt
Cook for 5 minutes. Cooking the carrots with the onions for a while builds flavour. Add:
   1.35 litres stock
Bring to the boil, lower the heat and simmer until the carrots are tender, about 30 minutes. When done, season with salt to taste, and purée if desired.

A SOUP OF MANY VEGETABLES

Minestrone means 'big soup' in Italian: a big soup of many vegetables. In order for them all to be cooked through at the same time, they're added in stages. First a tasty *soffritto* (a base of aromatic vegetables) is made, long-cooking vegetables are added and moistened with water or stock, and the soup is brought to the boil, at which point the more tender vegetables are added. Dried beans and pasta are cooked separately and added at the end. The recipe below is for a classic summertime minestrone, followed by seasonal variations.

The soffritto can be made of onions only but often includes carrots and celery. Fennel can be substituted for the celery when a more delicate flavour is wanted. Garlic is always added at the end of the cooking to ensure that it does not burn. Be sure to use a heavy-bottomed pot and lots of olive oil. For a more hearty soup, let the soffritto cook to a golden hue; for a less robust version, don't let the vegetables colour at all. Either way, the vegetables should be cooked through to give the soup the full benefit of their flavours; this will take 10 minutes or more. They're done when they look and taste good enough to eat on their own.

The vegetables added after the soffritto – such as squash and green beans – are cut into pieces small enough to ensure that each spoonful of soup will contain a mixture. They're added sequentially, according to the length of time they take to cook through without getting mushy. Greens need to be cut into bite-size pieces, too; if they're cut in strips they can hang down and dribble hot soup on your chin or your clothes. Winter greens such as kale or chard take longer to cook and should go in with the first group of vegetables. Tender greens such as spinach will cook in just a few minutes and should be added towards the end of cooking. Salt the soup as it cooks; this will intensify and improve the flavour as a last-minute salting cannot.

Dried beans – and pasta, if you're using it – should be cooked separately before being added to the soup. Save the bean cooking liquid; it adds flavour and body. The cooked beans should be added during the last 10 minutes so they have a chance to absorb flavour, but not overcook. The pasta should be added at the very end so it doesn't overcook and get bloated and flabby.

To preserve its fresh flavour, the garnish of olive oil and cheese should be added to the bowls of soup, not to the pot. I always pass a bowl of grated cheese and a bottle of olive oil at the table.

MINESTRONE
8 servings

Prepare:
   225g dried cannellini or borlotti beans (see p. 54)
This will yield 550 to 675g of cooked beans. Reserve the cooking liquid.
Heat in a heavy-bottomed saucepan over medium heat:
   50ml olive oil
Add:
   1 large onion, finely chopped
   2 carrots, peeled and finely chopped
Cook for 15 minutes, or until tender. Add:
   4 garlic cloves, peeled and coarsely chopped
   5 thyme sprigs
   1 bay leaf
   2 teaspoons salt
Cook for 5 minutes longer. Add, and bring to the boil:
   675ml water

When boiling, add:
>*1 small leek, diced*
>*225g French beans, cut into 2.5-cm lengths*

Cook for 5 minutes, then add:
>*2 medium courgettes, cut into small dice*
>*2 medium tomatoes, peeled, seeded and chopped*

Cook for 15 minutes. Taste for salt and adjust as necessary. Add the cooked beans, along with:
>*225ml bean cooking liquid*
>*About 450g spinach leaves, coarsely chopped*

Cook for 5 minutes. If the soup is too thick, add more bean cooking liquid. Remove the bay leaf.

Serve in bowls, each one garnished with:
>*2 teaspoons extra-virgin olive oil*
>*1 tablespoon or more grated Parmesan cheese*

Autumn Minestrone with Kale and Butternut Squash

Follow the recipe, but add 2 finely chopped celery stalks to the soffritto and cook to a rich golden brown. Instead of thyme, add about ½ teaspoon chopped rosemary and 1 teaspoon chopped sage with the garlic. Borlotti beans can be substituted for the cannellini beans. Omit the French beans, courgettes, fresh tomatoes and spinach, and use instead 1 bunch kale, stemmed, washed and chopped; 1 small can of tomatoes, drained and chopped; and ½ butternut squash, peeled and cut into 5-mm cubes. Cook the tomatoes and kale with the soffritto for 5 minutes, add the water, and cook for 15 minutes. Add the squash and continue cooking until tender, about 10 to 15 minutes, before adding the cooked beans.

Winter Minestrone with Turnips, Potatoes and Cabbage

Follow the recipe, but to the soffritto add 2 finely chopped celery stalks and cook to a rich golden brown. Cut up ½ head cabbage into bite-size pieces and cook until tender in salted boiling water. For the French beans, courgettes and tomatoes, substitute 450g turnips and 225g waxy potatoes, peeled and cut into bite-size pieces. If the turnips have fresh greens attached, stem, wash and chop them and add them to the soup with the turnips and potatoes. Towards the end of the cooking, add the beans and, instead of the spinach, the cooked cabbage.

Spring Minestrone with Peas and Asparagus

Instead of carrot in the soffritto, use 1 fennel bulb, trimmed and cut into bite-size pieces. Do not let it brown. If green garlic is available, use 2 or 3 stalks, trimmed and chopped, instead of garlic cloves. Use 2 leeks instead of one. Add the liquid (half water, half stock, if possible), bring to the boil and simmer for 10 minutes. Omit the French beans, courgettes and tomatoes. Substitute 175g shelled peas (from 450g in the pod) and 225g asparagus, trimmed and sliced on the diagonal into 1-cm-thick pieces. Add with the beans and cook for 5 minutes before adding the spinach. If not serving this soup right away, cool it down quickly in an ice bath so the asparagus does not lose its bright green colour.

Beans, Dried and Fresh

Beans belong to a huge botanical family that includes all the flowering plants whose fertilized flowers form pods, or shells, with seeds inside. These are the legumes; beans, peas, soybeans and lentils all fall into this family. After these plants bloom in spring, their pods grow and swell; and the seeds within ripen until, for a brief moment in time – no more than a few weeks – they reach full maturity and deliciousness before beginning to dry on the vine. The shells become dry and papery and the beans are ready to harvest. Green beans, of course, are consumed pod and all, although some varieties such as runner beans mature into very good shell beans when left on the vine to ripen. The recipes in this section, however, are about the so-called shell beans, or shelling beans: the dryable kinds that are removed from their shells and either cooked and eaten fresh, right at harvest; or else dried and stored, to be soaked and cooked later on.

SHELL BEANS

I cook shell beans in different ways: sometimes plain, with rosemary, garlic and olive oil; sometimes in soup, alone or with other vegetables, puréed or not; other times in gratins, under crunchy breadcrumbs. Beans can be cooked in advance, and they keep well for a day or two, refrigerated in their cooking liquid, to be reheated and served plain or incorporated into any number of dishes. What's more, beans are extremely nutritious and affordable compared to other sources of protein; and, perhaps best of all, little kids love them.

In late summer, from August through September, I look for the many varieties of fresh ripe shell beans that may be fleetingly available. They are a real treasure of the late summer and early fall. Unlike their dried counterparts, fresh shell beans do not need to be soaked and they cook quite quickly. And all winter long there are the many, many dried bean varieties to bring variety and colour to winter menus.

As time passes, beans continue to dry out. When soaked, a bean from a recent harvest will plump quickly and cook quickly, too. I find that dried beans are best bought in bulk; that way it's more likely they'll be from a recent harvest. Older beans take a lot longer to soak and cook and won't taste nearly as good. They often cook unevenly, with some turning to mush while others remain hard. If you can't find good organic beans in your area, talk to the produce manager at your supermarket. Talk to the farmers at your farmers' market. Let them know you're looking for beans.

BEAN VARIETIES

Here is a short list of varieties from among the astonishing array of available dried beans, lentils and peas. In my experience, old-fashioned bean varieties – those sold as heirloom varieties – are usually tastier than many of the more common varieties. Keep trying different ones in pursuit of your own personal favourites.

Cannellini beans are the white beans I use the most. Mild-flavoured, with a creamy texture, they are good for many Italian and French dishes. Other white beans include: haricots blancs, navy and lima beans.

Borlotti beans are light reddish brown with dark brown speckles. Plump and full-flavoured, they are the typical beans for *pasta e fagioli*, *ribollita* and other hearty Italian fare. They are found fresh in the late summer and fall and dried year-round. There are many similar bean varieties, with beautiful names: Eye of the Goat and Tongue of Fire, for example.

Flageolet beans are diminutive, light green beans with a distinctive vegetable flavour and a relatively firm texture. These are commonly paired with lamb and duck in French cuisine.

Lima beans are exquisite when fresh. Among the varieties I especially like, fresh and dried, is the huge brown-and-pink-speckled Christmas lima, which has a unique nutty flavour.

Pinto beans are a staple of Mexican and Tex-Mex cuisine. They're tasty either whole or fried in lard and crushed up. Many varieties have exceptional flavour, including Flor de Mayo, Flor de Junio and Rattlesnake beans.

Black beans are the mainstay of many Latin American cuisines. They have a wonderful earthy flavour that makes tasty soup, among other things, but they often take longer to cook than other beans.

Lentils are not true beans, exactly; they are tiny, lens-shaped pulses that belong to another species of dried legume, and come in many colours. They cook quickly and don't need to be soaked. There are many varieties, but the ones I use the most are small French green lentils and tiny black beluga lentils, which both hold their shape when cooked. I also love the yellow and red-orange lentils used in Indian cooking for soups and purées.

Black-eyed peas (and their cousins crowder peas) are ingredients in some classic American Southern dishes. Although hard to shell, they are well worth trying fresh. I love them in ragouts with French beans and herbs.

Chickpeas or garbanzo beans are hard and dense when dried and take a little longer to cook than other beans. In the late summer, you may be lucky enough to find fresh chickpeas, which are green and delicate. (The flour made from dried chickpeas makes many interesting dishes.)

Soybeans I cook fresh, in boiling salted water, and serve in their shells with sea salt sprinkled over (*edamame* in Japan). Eat them plain, popping the beans out of the pods into your mouth. They make a healthy and well-received snack for kids.

SOAKING AND COOKING BEANS

Dried beans cook best when soaked for a number of hours. Overnight is best. Cover the beans with plenty of water to keep them from poking up above the surface when they have absorbed water and swelled. I cover them with at least three times as much water as beans. If all the beans were not completely submerged overnight some will cook at a different rate than others and you'll end up with overdone and underdone beans in the same pot. Drain after soaking and use fresh water for cooking them.

All over the world, beans are traditionally cooked in earthenware pots (and for some reason they seem to taste better when they are), but any heavy nonreactive pot will do. Try to choose a wide pot so the layer of beans isn't too deep; otherwise the beans are hard to stir and the ones on the bottom of the pot get crushed. Be sure to use enough water so that stirring them is easy: the water level should always be a couple of centimetres above the level of the beans. If the water is too low, the beans will be crowded and will tend to fall apart when they are stirred. Worst of all, they might start to stick and burn on the bottom of the pot. Salt is best added towards the end of the cooking to keep the beans tender.

When done, the beans should be tender but not falling apart, though it is better to overcook them than under-cook them! You don't want them to be the least bit al dente, or crunchy. The best way to test them is to bite one. Start testing after an hour. When they are fully cooked, let the beans cool in their liquid before you drain them. If they're drained right away, the skins will crack and they'll look shaggy.

When cooking fresh shell beans there is no need to soak them. Just pop them out of their shells and put them into a pot. Cover with water by no more than about 3.5cm: the beans will not absorb much water. Add the salt at the beginning and begin testing for doneness after about 10 minutes. Depending on the variety, the beans may take as long as an hour to cook, but usually they are done in much less time.

Beans can be flavoured at the end of their cooking and served right away; or once cooked, they can be cooled, flavoured or not, refrigerated (or frozen) in their liquid, and used later.

WHITE BEANS WITH ROSEMARY AND GARLIC
Makes 675g beans

Soak overnight in 1 litre water:
> *175g dried white beans (cannellini, haricots blancs, navy, and so on)*

Drain and transfer to a heavy pot. Add water to cover by 5cm. Bring to the boil. Lower the heat and skim off any foam. Simmer gently for 2 hours or so, until the beans are tender. Add more water if necessary during the cooking. Season to taste with:
> *Salt*

In a heavy-bottomed saucepan or frying pan, warm over low heat:
> *50ml extra-virgin olive oil*

Add:
> *4 garlic cloves, peeled and coarsely chopped*
> *1 teaspoon coarsely chopped rosemary leaves*

Cook just until the garlic is soft, about 2 minutes. Stir

into the beans, taste for salt and adjust as needed. Let the dish sit for a few minutes before serving to allow the flavours to marry.

FLAVOURING BEANS

Beans cooked and served simply seasoned – like the cannellini beans in the previous recipe with garlic and rosemary – is only one of a great many bean dishes – soups, gratins, purées and more – that are tastier when their primary flavouring comes after an initial cooking. I sometimes add garlic or herbs or even a bit of onion while the beans are cooking the first time, but I find that good flavour is most prominent when it's added after the primary cooking. Added flavour can mean anything from a dash of olive oil to a complex tomato sauce, depending on the dish. For example, in the classic Italian dish called *fagioli all'uccelletto* (which means beans seasoned like a small bird), the cooked beans are simmered in a garlicky tomato sauce with plenty of sage. An example from Mexican cuisine is *frijoles refritos*, beans which, after an initial cooking, are fried in lard with garlic and sautéed onions, and then mashed. (There are exceptions to every rule, and one that comes immediately to mind is that when something like a ham hock or a prosciutto bone is used to flavour beans, it can be added at the beginning to cook slowly with the beans throughout their cooking.)

The beans should be drained of most of their liquid before final flavourings are added. (Save the bean water to make a tasty soup base or to moisten a gratin as it cooks.)

Once the beans are ready, stir in the flavourings. Continue to cook them together for at least 10 minutes or so, to allow the flavours to infuse the beans.

FRESH BROAD BEANS

Broad beans are a harbinger of spring. Like other kinds of beans, they form in pods, but they are also covered in a tough, rather bitter skin. The earliest harvests offer beans that are tiny, brilliant green and so tender they don't need to be peeled. When not eaten raw, straight from the pod, these are best cooked briefly with a little water and oil or butter. As the season progresses, the beans continue to mature, and they become larger and starchier. At this point they can be popped out of their pods, skinned and cooked into a luscious, bright green purée that I adore slathering on crisp croutons or serving alongside roasted meats. Still later in the season the beans turn yellow and dry out and are too mature to use this way.

Broad beans do require a bit of preparation, but their delicate taste and splash of colour are well worth the effort. Popping the beans from their thick soft pods is an enjoyable group project that even little children can join. An easy way to pop the beans out of the pod is to grasp one with both hands; bend the pod back against your thumbs and press out, snapping the beans out of the pod. After the beans are shelled the opaque outer skin of the bean needs to be removed. (Although in Mediterranean cooking the skins are sometimes left on, this increases the cooking time and results in a different taste.) To do so, plunge the beans into boiling water and leave them until the skin is easy to remove. This will take less than a minute, so check one right away. (If you cook the beans too long they will get mashed when you try to slip them out of their skins.) Drain the beans and put them into a bowl of ice water. When they are cool, drain them, and pop out the beans, using a fingernail to slit the skin and squeezing the bean out with the fingers of the other hand.

Don't cook the skinned beans too quickly; medium-low heat is best. Stir them occasionally as they are cooking, and, if you notice that they are drying out, add a little water. They are done when they can be crushed into a smooth paste when pressed with a spoon.

All kinds of beans, fresh or dried, can be flavoured and made into tasty purées. I love cannellini bean purée, and refried pinto beans, too. Another favourite hors d'oeuvre is chickpeas with olive oil and hot pepper puréed and served with flatbread or crackers.

BROAD BEAN PURÉE
Makes about 675g

Bring a pot of water to the boil as you shell the beans from:

   1.8kg broad beans

Blanch quickly in the boiling water and then cool in ice water. Drain and pop the beans out of their skins.
Heat in a heavy-bottomed saucepan:

   100ml olive oil

Add the broad beans with:

   4 garlic cloves, peeled and sliced
   1 branch rosemary

Salt

100ml water

Cook until the broad beans are very tender, stirring occasionally, and adding more water as necessary. The beans are done when they can be crushed easily with the back of a spoon, about 15 minutes. Mash with a spoon or pass them through a food mill.

Stir in:

50ml extra-virgin olive oil

Taste and season with salt as needed. Thin with water if necessary. Serve right away or at room temperature.

Pasta and Polenta

Pasta and polenta are two of the great standbys of the pantry and two of the great mainstays of the Italian table. A box of dried pasta and a few other staples can always be turned into a quick meal without much planning; and polenta, which is simply corn ground into cornmeal, is also remarkably versatile and exceptionally tasty. Pasta and polenta are prepared similarly, in salted boiling water; and at their simplest, both can be served with little more than butter or oil and some cheese. I like to make fresh pasta, too, because its texture is particularly well suited to certain dishes such as baked lasagne and hand cut fresh noodles with a savoury meat sauce or stew, and it is essential for homemade ravioli and cannelloni.

MAKING FRESH PASTA

Fresh pasta, at least the version I make most often, is nothing more than flour and eggs. The prospect of making pasta may seem intimidating, but I assure you, it is surprisingly easy. The most time-consuming part is rolling it out, but a hand-cranked machine makes this job quick and easy. (Charity shops and car boot sales are great places to look for pasta machines.)

The main ingredient of pasta is flour. The flour I use most often is unbleached, organic and plain. (Bleached flour, besides having added chemicals, has very little flavour and makes a sticky dough.) For different flavours and textures, whole-grain flours such as whole wheat, buckwheat, farro and others can be substituted for up to half the amount of flour; more than that and the dough becomes friable or crumbly and can't be rolled as thin as needed for some recipes. Durum flour makes great pasta with a good bite but unfortunately it can be hard to find; if you do come across it, substitute it for up to half of the total flour. Semolina is ground from durum wheat, but it is very coarse and hard to turn into egg pasta. Experiment to see what your favourite flours and ratios are.

To make the dough by hand, measure the flour into a bowl, one that easily holds the flour with plenty of extra room for stirring. Break the eggs into another bowl or cup and beat them lightly to mix the yolks and whites. Make a well in the flour (use a spoon or your hand to make a depression) and pour in the beaten eggs. Use a fork to stir as though scrambling the eggs, scraping in flour from the sides bit by bit. When the egg and flour mixture gets too stiff to stir with a fork, continue mixing with your hands. When the flour is mostly absorbed, turn the dough out on to a lightly floured surface and knead lightly until it comes together. It won't be perfectly smooth. Wrap it in a polythene bag or clingfilm and let sit for an hour at room temperature (or longer, refrigerated). The dough needs to rest to allow the gluten that has been activated by the stirring and kneading to relax, making the dough easier to roll out.

To make the dough with a stand mixer, put the flour into the bowl, attach the paddle and slowly pour in the eggs while mixing at low speed. Mix until the dough begins to come together in small, moist clumps. Turn out on to a lightly floured surface and knead together. Cover and let rest as above.

Through trial and error I have discovered that a wetter dough is much easier to work with, especially when rolling out by hand (it does not spring back as quickly as a dry dough). The ideal texture for pasta is a dough that comes together easily but is not sticky. If, after mixing, the dough is crumbly and dry, moisten with a sprinkling of water. Add more as needed, a little at a time, but avoid making it *too* wet. If the dough is too wet and sticky, you can knead in more flour, but let it rest at least an hour to come together. Flour will vary from batch to batch, so what seemed like the perfect amount of liquid one time may be too much or too little another.

Pasta can be rolled by hand or with a machine. The rollers of the machine create perfectly smooth noodles, while hand-rolling results in interesting surface irregularities for the sauce to cling to, adding nuance and flavour. It's worth rolling the dough by hand once to taste and feel the difference.

When rolling pasta with a machine, first flatten the ball of dough with your hands, then open the machine up to its fullest setting, and, while cranking slowly but steadily, pass the dough through the rollers of the machine. (If you are making a large amount of dough, divide it into smaller balls to avoid overloading the machine.) Fold the rolled dough over itself into thirds, as though folding a letter, and put it through the machine again. This process kneads the dough. If the dough is sticking, sprinkle it lightly with flour. Smooth out the flour with your hand before rolling again. Fold and roll two more times; the dough should be soft and silky. If not, repeat the kneading one more time.

Once kneaded, the dough is ready to be stretched. Put it through the widest setting one more time, then lower the setting each time you put the dough through. As the dough begins to lengthen and thin, put your hand (the one that is not turning the crank) very, very lightly on top of the dough as it goes through the machine; this helps it to stay on course and not veer off and crumple up under the rollers. Keep track of the surface of the pasta; if it gets sticky, sprinkle lightly with flour again, smoothing the flour with your hand. (Any lumps of flour will make pits in the dough.) To deal with the pasta between rollings, fold the lengthening sheet of dough as it comes out of the machine, back and forth over itself. Then feed one end of the folded pasta through the rollers on the next thinnest setting and it will unfold as it is drawn through the machine.

Once the dough has reached the desired thickness, it's time to cut it. Bear in mind that pasta expands quite a bit as it cooks, so if you're unsure how thin to roll the dough, cut and cook a couple of trial noodles. If the noodles are just a bit too thick and only need a slight adjustment, run the pasta through the same setting again. Most pasta makers come with cutting attachments, but noodles are easy to cut by hand; they look charmingly handmade and have a pleasing irregular texture. Cut the dough into 30- to 40-cm-long sheets and stack these on top of each other, flouring generously between sheets. Fold the stack in half lengthwise, and then in half again. Cut across the stack to make noodles of the desired width. Toss with a bit of extra flour to unfold them (I love the way the noodles feel falling through my fingers), and spread on a plate or baking sheet. Cover with baking parchment or a light towel and refrigerate if not cooking right away. For lasagne, cannelloni, ravioli and other stuffed pasta, the sheets of pasta are cut into larger squares or left in long sheets to be stuffed.

Fresh pasta absorbs a lot of water, so it needs to be cooked in a generous amount of salted, rapidly boiling water. Stir to ensure that the noodles don't stick together. The pasta is done when the noodles are cooked through, but still have a good bite (in Italian, *al dente*, 'to the tooth'). Fresh pasta cooks very quickly, in 3 to 6 minutes, depending on the thickness of the noodles.

FRESH PASTA
4 servings

Measure and put into a bowl:
   200g flour
Mix together in another bowl:
   2 eggs
   2 egg yolks
Make a well in the flour and pour in the eggs. Mix with a fork, as though scrambling the eggs, incorporating the flour bit by bit. When the flour is too stiff to mix with a fork, finish the mixing by hand. Turn the dough out on to a floured surface and knead lightly. Or put the flour in a stand mixer fitted with the paddle attachment and pour

in the eggs while mixing at low speed. Mix until the dough just starts to come together, adding a few drops of water if the dough is dry and crumbly. Turn out and knead as above. Shape the dough into a disc and wrap in polythene. Let rest at least an hour before rolling.

Roll out by hand on a lightly floured board or using a machine. When using a machine, roll the pasta through the widest setting, fold into thirds, and pass through the machine again. Repeat two more times. Then roll, decreasing the setting on the machine one notch at a time, until the pasta is the desired thickness. Cut into noodles.

MAKING CANNELLONI AND RAVIOLI

For cannelloni roll out the pasta and cut the sheets into rectangles about 10 by 7.5cm. Cook in salted boiling water until done. Cool in a large bowl of cold water and lay the rectangles out on a cloth. Avoid stacking them; they will stick to one another unless you brush them first with olive oil or melted butter.

Pipe or spoon a bit of filling along one third of the length of a piece of pasta. Gently roll the pasta to form a large straw. Place the cannelloni seam side down in a buttered ovenproof pan. Bake them with sauce, stock or melted butter and cheese for 20 minutes in a preheated 200°C/400°F/gas 6 oven.

To make ravioli, roll out the pasta fairly thin and cut into sheets about 35cm long. Keep the stack of well-floured pasta sheets under a towel to prevent them from drying as you work with one sheet at a time. Pipe or spoon 1 tablespoon of filling along the lower third of a sheet of pasta. Keep about 3.5cm between each blob of filling. Spray very lightly with a fine mist of water. Fold the upper half of the pasta over the lower half; then, starting at the fold, gently coax all the air out of the ravioli, pressing the two layers of pasta together with your fingertips. When the sheet of ravioli has been formed and pressed, use a zigzag rolling cutter to cut off the bottom edge and to cut between each pocket of filling. Separate the ravioli and lay them out on a baking sheet sprinkled with flour; make sure they aren't touching one another or they will stick together. Cover with a towel or baking parchment and refrigerate until ready to cook. Keep refrigerated right up to the time of cooking to prevent the filling from seeping through the pasta, which can cause the ravioli to stick to the pan.

Cook the ravioli in salted boiling water for 5 to 6 minutes or until the pasta is done. Drain and place on a platter or in individual bowls. Sauce and garnish as desired.

COOKING DRY PASTA

Although spaghetti is a perennial favourite, there are lots of different noodle shapes and many different grain varieties that merit equal attention. Whichever you choose, proper cooking and saucing make all the difference. Here are a few tips to follow for a really great plate of pasta.

Water plays an important role in cooking and dressing pasta. Cook pasta in a large quantity of salted boiling water. As it cooks it absorbs the water and it will stick together if the noodles are crowded too tightly. Bring the water to a rolling boil before adding the noodles; this helps keep them moving instead of settling to the bottom of the pan. Stir them once or twice in the beginning to keep them from sticking to one another or to the pan. Salting the water seasons the noodles before they are sauced, making for a tastier dish. It is not necessary to put oil in the water. Doing so may help keep the noodles from sticking (which they won't anyway if there is enough boiling water in the pot), but the oily coating they receive while cooking prevents the sauce from adhering to the noodles in the bowl. And unless you are making a pasta salad, don't rinse the noodles after they are cooked: this takes away all the outer starch, which adds texture and flavour to the sauce.

Cook the pasta al dente: there should be no white core left in it but it should still be firm to the bite. Taste a noodle now and then to gauge the doneness; the white core is very apparent in a bitten piece of undercooked pasta. Dry egg noodles will cook fairly quickly (5 to 6 minutes) while more rustic noodles will take a lot longer (10 to 13 minutes). When the pasta is cooked, drain it right away to keep it from cooking further. Always save a little of the cooking water before draining; it can come in very handy when saucing the pasta.

There are a few different strategies for combining pasta with sauce. One is to put the drained pasta directly into the sauce and toss. (It is a good idea to season the noodles directly with a bit of salt before tossing them; this is especially true when a very simple sauce is being used.) Another is to toss the noodles with oil or butter and cheese and a little sauce, plate them and then top with more sauce – a good way to serve pasta with meat sauce. Yet another is to drain the pasta when it is a touch underdone and finish cooking it in the sauce for a few minutes. This only works with sauces that are juicy, as the pasta will continue to absorb liquid as it cooks. The pasta water that was saved when draining the noodles is very helpful for loosening thick sauces or stodgy noodles; it is full of flavour and texture from the salt and starch of the noodles and makes for a much lighter dish than adding more oil, butter or sauce.

Different noodles are better suited for certain sauces. Large chunky noodles go well with chunky sauces, egg noodles are good with buttery sauces or meat ragùs, and thin long noodles are complemented by simple tomato-based sauces as well as olive oil sauces like the one that follows.

SPAGHETTINI WITH OIL AND GARLIC
4 servings

Bring a large pot of salted water to the boil and cook until al dente:

450g spaghettini

Meanwhile, heat in a heavy-bottomed pan over medium-low heat:

75ml extra-virgin olive oil

When the oil is just warm, add:

4 garlic cloves, peeled and finely chopped
3 large parsley sprigs, stems removed, leaves chopped
A pinch of dried chilli flakes
Salt

Cook until the garlic is soft, turning off the heat just as the garlic starts to sizzle. Don't let it brown or burn.

Drain the pasta when cooked, reserving some of the cooking water. Add the noodles to the sauce in the pan with a pinch of salt and toss. Taste for seasoning and loosen with some of the cooking water if needed. Serve immediately.

MAKING POLENTA

Polenta is a very simple dish of ground corn cooked in water. It is exceptionally tasty and, like pasta, remarkably versatile. When first cooked, polenta is soft; as it cools, it becomes firm and can then be fried, barbecued or baked. Soft or firm, polenta is great next to roasted or braised meats, or sauced with a spoonful of tomato, meat or mushroom sauce. For variety, fresh sweetcorn or broad beans can be stirred into soft polenta. Polenta can be turned into a luscious torta by layering it with cooked vegetables, cheese and sauce. Whether ground from yellow or white corn, polenta is ground coarser than cornmeal but finer than grits (coarsely ground corn). When fresh it smells sweet and looks bright yellow. Like all grains, it should be stored in a cool, dark place and replaced when old.

Cook polenta in boiling water. The approximate ratio of water to grain is four to one. This will vary depending on the variety of corn, how coarse it is ground and how fresh it is; each batch you buy may be slightly different. Choose a heavy-bottomed pot when cooking polenta to avoid sticking and burning; use a flame tamer if a heavy pot is not available. Bring the water to a rolling boil and add the polenta in a slow, steady stream while stirring constantly with a whisk. Turn the heat down and continue whisking for 2 or 3 minutes, until the polenta is suspended in the water and no longer settles to the bottom of the pot. (This helps keep it from sticking to the bottom of the pan.) Season with salt and cook the polenta at a bare simmer, stirring occasionally, for about an hour. The polenta will be fully cooked and softened after 20 to 30 minutes, but the longer cooking time allows its full flavour to develop. Be warned that the thick polenta is very hot, so be careful when stirring and tasting. I spoon a bit on to a small plate to cool before tasting.

Polenta should have a pourable, creamy consistency. If the polenta becomes thick or stiff while cooking, add water as needed to maintain the proper consistency. If too much water is added by accident, and the polenta becomes thin and soupy, just keep cooking it to evaporate the water. Polenta will set quickly if not kept warm, so turn off the heat and cover the pot to keep it soft and hot for 20 minutes or so, or hold it for a longer time in a double boiler or by setting the pot in a larger pot of hot water. Polenta can be finished with butter or olive oil and cheese to enrich it and add flavour. Parmesan is the classic cheese to stir in, but try others; fontina, Cheddar or pecorino, for example. Mascarpone or blue cheese is a luxurious garnish to top a bowl of soft polenta.

To make firm polenta, spread hot soft polenta evenly on to a rimmed baking sheet (it is not necessary to oil the sheet). A depth of about 2.5cm works well for most purposes. Let the polenta sit at room temperature or refrigerate until set. Don't cover until it has cooled. The firm polenta can be cut into shapes to bake, barbecue or fry. To bake, brush with oil and bake in a preheated 180°C/350°F/gas 4 oven for 20 minutes or until crisp. To barbecue polenta, brush it with oil and place on a grill over hot coals; to prevent it from sticking, make sure the grill is hot. To fry, use shallow or deep fat. Polenta will always set when cooled, but both very thin polenta and polenta that has been finished with a lot of butter or oil can fall apart when barbecued or fried.

A polenta torta is made of alternate layers of polenta – either freshly made soft polenta or polenta that has already cooled and set – and sauce, such as tomato sauce, meat sauce or pesto; cooked greens or other vegetables; and cheese. A polenta torta is a great make-ahead dish, ready to heat up any time.

POLENTA
4 servings

Boil in a heavy-bottomed pot:
   900ml water
When boiling, whisk in:
   225g polenta
   1 teaspoon salt
Turn down the heat and stir constantly until the polenta is suspended in the water and no longer settles to the bottom of the pot. Cook for 1 hour, stirring occasionally, at a bare simmer. Add water if the polenta gets too thick. Stir in:
   3 tablespoons butter or olive oil
   50g grated Parmesan cheese

Taste and add more salt if needed. (Be careful when tasting the polenta; it is very hot.) Keep warm until ready to serve or spread it out on a rimmed baking sheet and let cool.

POLENTA TORTA
6 servings

Prepare:
  900g soft polenta (see above)
Prepare:
  450ml tomato sauce
Grate:
  100g Parmesan cheese
Slice about 5mm thick:
  225g fresh mozzarella (about 2 medium balls)

Oil an earthenware or other low-sided baking dish. Ladle in 300g soft polenta. Spread 225ml tomato sauce over the polenta. On top of the tomato sauce, arrange half of the mozzarella slices. Sprinkle with half the grated Parmesan cheese. Ladle over another 300g polenta, spread on the rest of the tomato sauce, layer on the rest of the mozzarella, then sprinkle with the rest of the Parmesan cheese. Ladle over the remaining polenta and allow the torta to sit for at least 30 minutes before baking to allow the polenta to set. Fifteen minutes before baking, preheat the oven to 180°C/350°F/gas 4. Bake until hot and bubbling, about 30 minutes.

Rice

A bowl of rice is as basic, as comforting and as adaptable to everyday eating as bread. There are more than 40,000 varieties of rice, all stemming from a single species, *Oryza sativa*, but they all fall, more or less, into one of two categories: short-grain or long-grain. The varieties with short, fat, starchy grains have traditionally been grown and eaten in Japan, Korea, parts of China and parts of Europe (the varieties grown for paella in Spain and for risotto in Italy are short-grain). The many long-grain varieties, which are relatively less sticky and have longer, thinner grains, include fragrant basmati rice from India, jasmine rice from Thailand, and Carolina rice from the United States.

COOKING PLAIN RICE

When harvested, every grain of rice, whether short or long, is surrounded by a layer of bran and encased within a husk, or hull. Rice with just the husks removed is called brown rice. When the bran layer of brown rice is milled and polished away, the result is white rice, which cooks more quickly, is less nutty-tasting and is much less chewy than brown rice. (What is known as wild rice is the nearly black seed kernel of another plant entirely, a wild North American aquatic grass.) Plain rice can be central to many a quick meal: a make-your-own-sushi dinner, for example, with a big bowl of warm short-grain Japanese sticky rice and a plate of sliced fish, thinly sliced carrots and cucumbers and sheets of crisp seaweed; or a thoroughly satisfying lunch of golden lentil soup flavoured with cumin and garlic and accompanied by delicate basmati rice.

Cooking plain rice used to seem mysteriously difficult to me, even though I knew objectively that it involves nothing more than cooking the dried grains of rice in liquid, covered or uncovered, until they are done. And, in fact, you can boil rice in a generous quantity of water and drain it when it's done, or you can use no more water than will both evaporate and be absorbed by the rice in the time it takes the rice to cook perfectly. Or you can use a combination of these methods. The trick is learning the correct ratios of water to rice.

When rice is cooked it can end up unpleasantly sticky, which is why certain varieties benefit from a preliminary washing to remove excess surface starch. (The kinds of rice used for risotto and paella are never washed, however; the extra starch is an essential ingredient in these dishes.) To wash rice, put it into a large bowl, add cold water to cover and swish the rice around, rubbing it between your hands now and then. When the water looks cloudy, pour it off (a strainer can be helpful here), and repeat the process until the rinsing water is clear or almost clear. Drain the rice well. If the recipe calls for soaking, this is the time to do it. Cover with water by at least 2.5cm (or with the amount of water specified in a recipe) and soak for the required time.

To cook rice by the simplest absorption method, measure rice and water into a pot, bring to the boil, immediately turn down to a simmer, cover the pot tightly and cook the rice until all the water is absorbed, about 15 to 20 minutes for white rice – and about 40 minutes for brown. Different kinds of rice absorb different quantities of liquid: 200g brown rice absorbs about 900ml of water; 200g long-grain white rice absorbs about 340ml; and 215g short-grain white rice absorbs only 225ml and 2 tablespoons of water. As in the second absorption method given here, many cooks add a pinch of salt and a teaspoon of butter or olive oil to every 200g rice, both for flavour and to help keep the grains from sticking together. Whichever method you use, when the rice is cooked, let it rest, covered, for 5 to 10 minutes before fluffing and serving it. It will be easier to fluff because the grains separate a bit when they have cooled down slightly.

How do you know if all the water has been absorbed? Although some people say this will ruin the rice, you can take off the lid and stir the rice to get a peek at the bottom of the pot. I assure you, you will not ruin the rice! If it is still wet, it probably needs to cook longer. If the bottom of the pot is dry, the rice is probably done. Taste a grain: if it is still too hard, and there's no more water in the pan, sprinkle a few tablespoons of warm water over the rice and keep cooking. If, on the other hand, the rice seems done but is still wet, take off the lid and cook until the water has evaporated.

To cook rice by boiling, for every 200g rice bring about a litre of salted water to the boil. Add the rice and cook at a rapid boil until the rice is tender but not mushy. If soaked first, white rice cooks in 6 to 7 minutes; unsoaked, it takes 10 to 12. Brown rice takes much longer, at least 30 minutes. When cooked, drain the rice well and toss with salt, if needed, and a bit of butter or olive oil.

Yet another way to cook rice is a combination of the absorption and the boiling methods. Boil rice in a generous amount of water for 6 or 7 minutes, until almost tender; drain and return to the pot with butter or oil; cover tightly and bake in a hot oven for an additional 15 to 20 minutes. This makes relatively dry, fluffy rice that can be kept nicely warm.

PLAIN RICE: ABSORPTION METHOD ONE
3 to 4 servings

Rinse or wash:

215g short-grain rice

Drain well and put into a heavy-bottomed saucepan with:

225ml plus 2 tablespoons cold water

Cover and bring to the boil over medium-high heat. Immediately turn the heat down to low and cook until all the water is absorbed, about 15 minutes. Turn off the heat and let rest, still covered, for another 10 minutes. Fluff and serve.

PLAIN RICE: ABSORPTION
METHOD TWO
3 to 4 servings

Wash well in a few changes of water:
   200g basmati or other long-grain rice
Put into a heavy saucepan with:
   A pinch of salt
   450ml water
Set aside to soak for 30 minutes. When ready to cook, add:
   1 tablespoon butter
Bring to the boil and cook, uncovered, until the water is absorbed and the surface of the rice is covered with steam holes. Turn the heat to low and cover tightly. Cook for 7 minutes. Turn off the heat and let sit for 10 minutes. Stir gently to fluff and serve.

BOILED AND BAKED
LONG-GRAIN RICE
3 to 4 servings

Wash well in a few changes of water:
   200g basmati or other long-grain rice
Cover with water by 2.5cm, and soak for about 20 minutes. In a heavy-bottomed pot, bring to the boil:
   2 litres salted water
Drain the rice, add it to the boiling water and cook for 6 to 7 minutes. Test for doneness. The grains should be

slightly al dente, or hard in the centre. Drain well and mound back into the pot. Heat until just melted:

2 tablespoons butter

1½ tablespoons milk or water

Pour the butter mixture over the rice and cover the pot tightly with kitchen foil or a tight-fitting lid. Bake in a preheated 180°C/350°F/gas 4 oven for 15 minutes until dry and fluffy.

MAKING PILAF

A pilaf is a savoury dish of rice that has first been sautéed in fat and then cooked in a seasoned liquid. (It differs from a risotto in that the liquid is entirely absorbed.) Depending on the recipe, a pilaf may also include nuts, spices, a few vegetables or even a complex meat stew. I make mostly simple pilafs, such as the red rice pilaf that follows, to go with quesadillas and black beans, or a basmati rice pilaf with saffron and onions to eat with a vegetable ragout. Long-grain rice is usually used in pilafs, although some cuisines use short-grain rice.

Sautéing the rice before adding the liquid enriches the flavour of the dish and coats each grain in fat. This, along with thorough washing, keeps the rice from sticking together or clumping. Olive oil and butter are the most commonly used fats. To avoid burning the butter while sautéing the rice, add a little oil to it, or use clarified butter.

Onion is usually sautéed for a few minutes in the fat before the rice is added. After the rice is sautéed, a flavourful liquid is poured over it and brought to the boil.

The pilaf is simmered, covered, until all the liquid has been absorbed, about 15 minutes. Depending on their cooking times, vegetables and meats are added sometimes with the liquid, sometimes after the rice has been cooking for a while. The tomato in the red rice pilaf here is added at the beginning to colour the rice evenly. When done, pilafs should be allowed to rest for about 10 minutes before serving.

RED RICE PILAF
3 to 4 servings

In a heavy-bottomed pot heat:
   1½ tablespoons olive oil
Add and cook over medium heat until translucent, about 5 minutes:
   1 small onion, finely diced
Stir in and cook for 5 minutes:
   200g long-grain rice, rinsed and drained
Add:
   2 garlic cloves, finely chopped
   1 small tomato, peeled, seeded and finely chopped (or 2
      plum tomatoes, canned or fresh)
   ½ teaspoon salt (less, if using seasoned stock)
   2 tablespoons coarsely chopped coriander
Stir and cook for 1 or 2 minutes. Pour in:
   340ml chicken stock or water
Bring to the boil, turn the heat down to low and cover tightly. Cook until all the liquid is absorbed and the rice is tender, about 15 minutes. Turn off the heat and let rest, covered, for 10 minutes before serving.

MAKING RISOTTO

Risotto is Italian comfort food, a luscious dish of tender rice in its own creamy sauce. Considered by many to be labour-intensive restaurant fare, risotto is actually a basic one-pot dinner that pleases everyone. Risotto is made from starchy short-grain rice, which, when moistened with successive additions of stock, gains concentrated flavour and a distinctive saucy texture.

Of the special short-grain rice varieties that have been developed in northern Italy specifically for risotto the best known is Arborio; others are Vialone Nano (an extra-short-grain rice), Baldo and my favourite, Carnaroli. All these varieties have short, plump grains that can absorb a lot of liquid while retaining some textural integrity (the grains are said to have a good bite), with abundant superficial starch to make the risotto creamy.

Because the rice for a risotto is cooked in fat before any stock is added, use a heavy-bottomed pot, preferably stainless steel or enamelled cast iron, or the rice will scorch too easily. Pick a pot with relatively high sides (but not so high that stirring is difficult and evaporation is inhibited) and a diameter that is wide enough so that when the raw rice is added it's between 5mm and 1cm deep in the pot.

The first step is to make a flavourful base of sautéed diced onions. The onion is cooked until soft in a generous amount of fat (usually butter, but olive oil, beef marrow and even bacon fat are sometimes used). Once the onions are soft the rice is added and sautéed for a few minutes. In Italian this is called the *tostatura*, or 'roasting'. The idea is to coat and seal each grain of rice. The rice will begin to sizzle and turn translucent, but it should not colour or brown. At this point, some white wine is added, for fruit and acidity. For 325g of rice, I use about 100ml of wine, but I never bother to measure it exactly; I simply pour in enough wine to reach the top of the rice, without covering it. This works for any quantity of rice and is much easier than trying to make a calculation. Adding the wine before the stock gives it time to reduce and lose its raw alcohol flavour. Red wine or even beer can be substituted. When you are caught without a bottle of wine, a teaspoon or so of tasty wine vinegar added to the first addition of stock will approximate the acidity of wine.

After the wine is absorbed, stock is added. I use light chicken stock most often, but vegetable, mushroom and shellfish stocks also make lovely risottos. Keep in mind that your risotto will only be as good as the stock you use to make it. Unseasoned or lightly seasoned stocks are best. Many recipes say to keep the stock simmering (in its separate pan) the whole time the risotto is cooking. This isn't necessary; in fact, I prefer not to. The longer the stock simmers, the more it reduces, and its flavour can become too strongly concentrated. I bring the stock to the boil while the onions are cooking and then turn it off. The stock stays plenty warm.

The first addition of stock should just cover the rice. Adjust the heat to maintain a constant, fairly vigorous simmer. It is not necessary to stir constantly, but the risotto needs to be attended to frequently, and it certainly cannot be left on its own. When the level of liquid has dropped low enough that the rice is exposed, add more stock to cover. The stock should never be allowed to evaporate completely; the starch will coagulate and burn. Keep adding the stock in small increments; the rice should neither be flooded nor be allowed to dry out.

Season the rice with salt early on. My personal rule is to salt the risotto when I make the second addition of stock. This allows the salt to penetrate the grains of rice while they are cooking. The amount of salt needed will depend on the saltiness of the stock you're using.

From the time the rice is added to the onion, a risotto takes 20 to 30 minutes to cook. Taste it often to keep track of the seasoning and the state of the rice as it cooks. The final addition of stock is the deciding factor of the consistency of the risotto. Too much liquid, and the risotto will be soupy and overdone; too little, and it will be stodgy and underdone. It is easy to add more stock but difficult to take it out.

When the rice is nearly done and ready for its last addition of stock, stir in at the same time a pat of butter and a handful of grated Parmesan cheese. Give the pot a good stir, turn off the heat, and let it sit for a couple of minutes – this procedure, called the *mantecatura*, is the grand finale that develops the starch into wonderful creaminess. The risotto should be perfectly cooked, the rice tender with the suggestion of a bite (but not white at the core), and the sauce around it loose, but not too soupy. Serve it right away and leave it uncovered, as the rice will otherwise continue to absorb liquid and cook, even with the heat off.

Risotto bianco, or plain white risotto, delicious on its own, is also a blank canvas on to which almost anything can be painted in the foreground: meats, vegetables, seafood, other cheeses, and more. A good rule of thumb to follow when adding raw ingredients is to add them at twice the normal cooking time. For example, peas or prawns, which take 4 to 5 minutes to cook in boiling water, should be added to risotto 10 minutes before it is done, when the rice is a little more than half-cooked. Long-cooking vegetables such as carrots can be sautéed with the onions. Vegetable purées and vegetables and meats that have been cooked apart can be stirred in at the end. Mushrooms can be sautéed and added in two stages: early on, to flavour the stock, and at the end, to provide bites of contrasting flavour and texture. Add saffron and the stronger herbs with the onions, but stir in tender herbs just before serving. Citrus zest can be added in two stages, like mushrooms; when added in quantity, it should be blanched ahead. Some risottos, especially those made with shellfish, do not require cheese at the end.

RISOTTO BIANCO
4 servings

Melt in a heavy-bottomed 2.5- to 3-litre saucepan over medium heat:

 2 *tablespoons butter*

Add:

 1 *small onion, peeled and finely diced*

Cook until the onion is soft and translucent, about 10 minutes.

Add:

340g risotto rice (Arborio, Carnaroli, Baldo or Vialone Nano)

Cook the rice, stirring now and then, until translucent, about 4 minutes. Do not let it brown.

Meanwhile, in a separate pan, bring to the boil and then turn off:

1 litre chicken stock

Pour over the sautéed rice:

100ml dry white wine

Cook, stirring fairly often, until all the wine is absorbed. Add 225ml of the warm chicken stock and cook at a vigorous simmer, stirring occasionally. When the rice starts to get thick, pour in another 100ml of the stock and add some salt (how much depends on the saltiness of the stock). Keep adding stock, 100ml at a time, every time the rice thickens. Do not let the rice dry out. After 12 minutes, start tasting the rice, for doneness as well as for seasoning. Cook until the rice is tender but still has a firm core, 20 to 30 minutes in all. The final addition of stock is the most important: add just enough to finish cooking the rice without leaving it soupy. When the rice is just about done stir in:

1 tablespoon butter

40g grated Parmesan cheese

Stir vigorously to develop the creamy starch. Turn off the heat, let sit for 2 minutes, and serve. Add a splash of stock if the rice is too thick.

Tarts, Savoury and Sweet

A buttery crust with a savoury or sweet filling, a tart is a perfect food in the same way a sandwich or a pizza is. My favourite kind of tarts are the flat, crusty, round and open-faced versions known as galettes. The pastry shell is rolled quite thin, topped with a filling of fruit or vegetables (only about twice as thick as the shell) and baked free-form. The galette is baked until it is crisp and golden and the topping is softened, its flavours concentrated – an ideal marriage of textures and flavours.

MAKING SHORTCRUST PASTRY

The pastry determines the outcome of any tart: how it's made, how it's rolled out and how long it's cooked. The shortcrust I make most often is good for both savoury and sweet tarts and it makes good pie crust, too. Simply made with flour, butter and water, the pastry is tender, flaky and crisp. I avoided making shortcrust for years; I found it difficult to make, and I was often disappointed with the results. Then a friend who is an excellent pastry chef explained patiently just how the flour, butter and water work together, and after a little practice I began to get a feel for the *feel* of the dough, and the look of it, and my tarts got to be consistently good.

Flour contains a mixture of proteins known as gluten.

When mixed with water, these proteins are activated and begin to form a molecular network that makes dough elastic. The more a dough is stirred, or worked, the more the gluten is developed. Gluten is good for bread, which needs a strong supporting network in order to rise, but not so good for tarts: the more the dough is worked, the tougher the pastry will be. That's why it's important not to overwork shortcrust or knead it. Plain flour is the best flour to use for this recipe; strong bread flour is too high in gluten and so-called pastry flour and cake flour are too low (which makes the pastry mealy). Plain flour has just the right amount of gluten to give the dough a flaky texture. This is where the butter comes in.

Butter adds flavour and richness to the pastry and has important effects on texture as well. When butter is mixed in, it coats some of the flour, isolating the flour from the water – which slows down the activation of gluten, making the pastry more tender. When some of the butter is left in larger, uneven pieces and flattened by rolling, it will *steam* during baking, separating sheets of gluten from one another and creating a flaky texture. The more butter, the more tender the dough. The more irregular the sizes of the pieces of butter, the flakier the pastry.

When it's mixed into the flour, the butter should be quite cold – refrigerator temperature. If it gets too soft or melts, it makes the dough oily. Have all the ingredients ready before you start: butter chilled and cut into roughly 5-mm cubes, flour measured, water ice cold. Work the butter into the flour quickly, using your fingertips. If you have one of those tools called a pastry blender, so much the better. The important thing is to work quickly, lightly rubbing the butter and flour together with your fingertips, or chopping and mixing with the pastry blender, for about a minute. (You can use a stand mixer, too, fitted with the paddle attachment, and mix for about a minute at medium-low speed.) Now it's time to add the water.

The water's function is to hydrate the flour, thus activating the gluten. You need enough water to make a cohesive dough that is neither crumbly nor sticky. A dry, crumbly dough is hard to roll out and mealy to eat; wet, sticky dough makes tough pastry. The properties of both flour and butter vary, so the amount of ice-cold water you need to add will also vary. Measure out the amount called for, but don't pour it in all at once. Start by adding about three quarters of the amount. Stir and toss the dough with a fork as you dribble in the water. Avoid working the dough or squeezing it together. (If using a mixer, pour the water down the sides of the bowl while the machine is on low speed, mixing for 30 seconds or less.) Add water until the dough is *just* starting to clump together – if it forms a ball it's too wet. Test it by squeezing together a small handful. If it holds together, there's enough water; if the mass is dry and crumbly, it needs more. Add more water a few drops at a time, stirring lightly between additions.

When the dough is the right consistency, gently bring it together into a shaggy ball, working quickly with your fingers (the palms of your hand are much warmer than your fingertips). When making more than one ball of dough, separate the dough into equal parts before forming the balls. Wrap the ball(s) in clingfilm. (This is a great way to reuse polythene bags from the supermarket.) Once a ball of dough is wrapped in clingfilm, give it a good squeeze to compact it and flatten it into a disc, pinching the sides together to seal up any cracks that may have formed. Sealing the cracks makes it easier to roll the dough out later. Put the clingfilm-wrapped discs into the refrigerator to rest for at least an hour before you roll them out. A rest allows the moisture level in the dough to equalize and the gluten to relax, which make it easier to roll out the dough. The dough can be kept in the refrigerator for 2 days, and in the freezer for 2 months. Thaw frozen dough overnight in the refrigerator before using.

SHORTCRUST PASTRY
*Makes two 300-g balls of dough, enough for two
27.5-cm tarts or one double-crust 22.5-cm pie*

Have measured:
   100ml ice-cold water
Mix together:
   200g plain unbleached flour
   ½ teaspoon salt (omit if using salted butter)
Add:
   175g cold butter, cut into small (5-mm) cubes
Cut or work the butter into the flour with a pastry blender or your fingertips, leaving some of the butter in fairly large, irregular pieces. This will take 1 or 2 minutes. (Or mix for no more than a minute, at medium-low speed, in a stand mixer fitted with the paddle attachment.) Pour

in three quarters of the water, stirring all the while with a fork until the dough begins to form clumps. (In the mixer, turn the speed to low and pour the water down the sides of the bowl, mixing for 30 seconds or less.) Keep adding water if needed. Divide the dough in two, bring each part together into a ball, and wrap each ball in clingfilm. Compress each ball, and then flatten them into discs. Let rest, refrigerated, for 1 hour or longer.

ROLLING OUT SHORTCRUST PASTRY

Shortcrust pastry is easiest to roll out when it is malleable, but not soft. If it has been chilling for a number of hours, take it out of the refrigerator for about 20 minutes to soften. This may take more or less time depending on the room's temperature. Choose a surface to roll the dough on that is smooth and cool and where there is enough room to roll out the dough comfortably.

When ready to roll, take the disc of dough, still wrapped in clingfilm, and flatten it well with your hands, tapping or pinching the edges to seal shut any cracks that may appear. Dust the work surface lightly and evenly with flour, unwrap the dough and place it in the middle. Dust the top of the dough generously with flour as well. With the rolling pin, tap firmly across the top of the dough a few times to flatten the disc even more, then begin to roll. Guide the rolling pin from the centre of the disc towards the edges, pressing with firm but consistent pressure. After a few rolls, turn the dough over, smooth the flour on the top of the dough, lift it up and reflour the board. As the dough spreads out, be sure to close up any cracks that appear at the edges by pinching them together. You want the dough to flow out smoothly from under the rolling pin. As the circle gets bigger, keep guiding the rolling pin out from the centre, as opposed to rolling back and forth. Think of the dough as a bicycle wheel, and the spokes as the lines to follow while rolling. Give the dough a quarter turn now and then to keep it from sticking, dusting with flour as needed underneath or on top.

If the dough does start to stick, use a pastry scraper to slide gently underneath the edges and loosen the dough from the work surface. Carefully fold the dough back and throw some more flour over the work surface. (It's okay to use plenty of flour; just brush it off at the end.) Unfold the dough and slide it a little to make sure that it is well floured and moving freely. Finish rolling out the dough evenly. Check it for any thick spots and even these areas out.

Roll the dough a little less than 2mm thick for an open-faced tart. Roll it slightly thicker for a pie or double-crusted tart. Once the dough is rolled, brush off all the extra flour with a soft brush (a kitchen towel will work, if used with a light touch). To move the dough, fold it in half and then in quarters; this keeps it from stretching and tearing when lifted. Transfer the dough on to a baking sheet lined with baking parchment and unfold it. (The baking parchment ensures that the tart will not stick. I highly recommend using it.) Another way to transfer the dough is to roll it on to the rolling pin, then unroll it on to the parchment. Put the dough back into the refrigerator, baking sheet and all, to firm up before filling and finishing. If you are rolling out another piece of pastry, brush the flour evenly back over the work surface to reuse. Don't stack the pieces of rolled-out dough on top of each other. Separate them with baking parchment or put them on separate baking sheets.

To prebake a tart or pie shell 'blind' (without a filling), line the shell with a piece of kitchen foil or baking parchment, then fill the tart with a layer of dried beans reserved for this purpose (or other pie weights). Bake in a preheated 190°C/375°F/gas 5 oven for 15 minutes, or until lightly golden around the edge. Take the tart out of the oven and remove the foil and the weights. Return to the oven and cook for another 5 to 7 minutes, until the tart is an even light golden brown.

SAVOURY TARTS

There is a long list of variations of savoury galettes and most of them begin with sautéed onions. Sautéed onions are the perfect foil for the crisp, buttery crust of a tart. When combined with other vegetables, onions add protective moisture and deep flavour as the tart bakes in the oven. The pastry can also be rolled into long thin rectangular tarts, which can be cut into small pieces that make very popular finger food for a party.

Surprisingly, onions vary quite a bit, and not just in appearance. Sometimes they cook quickly and are so juicy they need to be drained before they can be used; other times they take a long time to soften and don't give off any liquid to speak of. Onions with very thin skins are usually much more sweet and juicy, while those with very hard, dark, golden skins tend to take longer to cook. All onions will eventually soften and be delicious, but when given the choice, I recommend selecting large onions that have a delicate, thin, lighter skin. Sweet Spanish onions make excellent tarts, baking up almost as sweet as honey. In the spring there are fresh onions, or spring onions, that have not been dried and cured, and still have their green stalks attached. Peel them and trim off their stalks, slice them thickly and cook until just soft. The flavour of spring onions is delicate and less sweet than that of mature cured onions.

The right amount of onions cooked to the right consistency is what makes a good tart. Pile the onions into a low-sided, heavy-bottomed pan with a generous amount of fat, and cook them slowly with herbs until soft and tasty; this will take at least 30 minutes. The onions must be cooled before they are spread on to the pastry or they will melt the butter before the tart bakes. The onions should be moist but not dripping wet or the tart will be soggy. If the onions are too juicy, drain them. Save the juice; it can be reduced and served with the tart as a little sauce or added to a vinaigrette.

If the onions are still juicy, even after draining, sprinkle a little flour over the pastry (avoiding the border), before adding the onions, to soak up some of the juice while the tart cooks. Bake on the lowest rack of the oven for a crust that is crisp and golden brown on the bottom. Check the underside by gently lifting up the tart with a spatula. When the tart is fully baked, slide it off the pan on to a cooling rack to rest. If left on the baking sheet to cool, it will steam and the pastry will not stay crisp.

Once you have mastered a basic onion tart, there are many variations you can try: add sliced sweet or hot peppers to the sautéing onions about halfway through cooking; grate some summer squash and stir it into the onions during their last few minutes of sautéing; or, before you fill the tart, while the onions are cooling, stir in either seasoned cherry tomato halves or roasted, peeled and sliced peppers. You can also top the layer of onions with sliced tomatoes or lightly grilled slices of aubergine. For a sweet and savoury tart, mix chopped roasted figs into the onions. Other variations include sprinkling the pastry with grated cheese or brushing it with a slurry of chopped herbs and olive oil before spreading on the onions. Artichoke hearts also can either be sautéed and stirred into the onions, or sliced and baked and arranged on top of them; when the tart comes out of the oven, try painting it with garlic and herb butter. And most of the year you can mix the onions with sautéed greens – chard, spinach, purple sprouting broccoli, or mustard. Or when the tart has only 10 minutes left to bake, top it with anchovies and black olives.

ONION TART
8 servings

Heat in a low-sided heavy-bottomed pan:
  4 tablespoons olive oil or butter
Add:
  6 medium onions (about 900g), peeled and thinly sliced
  3 thyme sprigs

Cook over medium heat until soft and juicy. This will take from 20 to 30 minutes. Season with:

> Salt

Cook for a few minutes more. Put into a bowl to cool. If the onions are very juicy, pour them into a strainer over a bowl to drain. Remove the liquid.

Roll out into a 35-cm circle:

> One 300-g disc of Shortcrust Pastry (p. 90)

Brush off the excess flour, transfer the dough to a baking sheet lined with baking parchment, and let it firm up in the refrigerator for 10 minutes or so. Spread the cooled onions over the dough (removing the thyme branches as you go), leaving a 3.5-cm border around the whole circumference of the dough. Fold the border up over the onions. For a shiny, more finished look, mix together and brush the folded dough rim with:

> 1 egg
>
> 1 tablespoon milk or water

Bake on the bottom rack of a preheated 190°C/375°F/gas 5 oven for 45 to 50 minutes, or until the crust is golden brown on the bottom. Slide the tart off the sheet on to a rack to cool. Serve warm or at room temperature.

FRUIT TARTS

When it is time for dessert, I like to eat fruit. A simple piece of ripe fruit is what I would choose first, but fruit tarts are irresistible, too. Almost any fruit can be made into a tart, either alone or in combination with others. Apples, pears, plums, apricots, peaches, nectarines, cranberries, quince, raspberries, blackberries – all are ideal, and the list goes on and on.

Fruit is best used when ripe – but not so ripe that it is getting soft. Don't hesitate to use bruised or blemished fruit; just discard the damaged parts. With the exception of berries and cherries (which are usually left whole and pitted), the fruit is cut before using. Apricots and small plums (pits removed) and figs can be cut in half and placed cut side up on the pastry. Larger plums and nectarines are better sliced thin. Peaches, apples and pears should be peeled, pitted or cored and then sliced. Some fruits, such as quince and dried fruit, need to be poached – gently cooked in sweet syrup – before being sliced and arranged on a tart. Rhubarb can be cut into matchsticks or slices. For best results the fruit should be sliced between 5 and 8mm thick.

Arrange the fruit on the pastry, leaving a 3.5-cm border. The fruit can be scattered evenly over the dough or it can be placed neatly in concentric circles. Apples and other drier fruit should be arranged tightly in overlapping circles. Juicy fruit such as plums and peaches should be one layer deep. Either way, the fruit should be fitted snugly together, one piece placed close to the next, because it will shrink as it cooks. Juicy fruit will give off more liquid as it cooks, making the crust soggy. There are a few things that can be done to mitigate this. The easiest is to scatter a tablespoon or two of flour over the pastry before arranging the fruit on top. Only sprinkle it on the part where the fruit will be arranged, not on the border. The flour can be mixed with sugar, chopped nuts or ground spices for more flavour. Another way to create a barrier between the pastry and the juice is to spread frangipane (a mixture of almond paste, sugar and butter) over the pastry; 100g is about the right amount for a single tart. Two to three tablespoons of jam can also be spread on to the pastry. This works best for fruit that's only slightly juicy.

Fold the border of dough up over the fruit and brush it generously with melted butter. Sprinkle with sugar, using up to 2 tablespoons. Lightly sprinkle the top of the fruit with more sugar: most fruit will only need 2 or 3 tablespoons. Rhubarb, tart plums and apricots are exceptions and need a lot more sugar than the others. Taste the fruit as you are assembling the tart. The sweeter it is, the less sugar it will need. Once assembled, the tart can be kept in the refrigerator or freezer until time to bake. It is nice to put a tart into the oven as you are sitting down to dinner: that way it will be ready in time for dessert, still warm from the oven. Bake the tart on the bottom rack of the oven until the bottom of the crust is golden brown. As with savoury tarts, it is important that the bottom of the pastry get brown and crisp.

Here are a few suggestions for embellishing any simple fruit tart: after the tart has baked for 30 minutes, sprinkle it with soft berries such as raspberries, loganberries or blackberries (first tossed with a little sugar) – this way the berries cook but don't get dried out. Currants, sultanas or raisins can be scattered over the crust before arranging the fruit. (If the raisins are very dry, soak them in water and Cognac, then drain them well before putting them on the tart.) And try sprinkling chopped candied citrus peel over the tart when it comes out of the oven.

For added gloss and flavour, glaze the tart after baking. If the fruit is juicy enough, the juice that pools around the fruit during baking can be brushed back over it – a bit like basting a roast with its own juices. A baked fruit tart can also be brushed with a little heated jam, with or without the fruit strained out.

APPLE TART
8 servings

Preheat the oven to 200°C/400°F/gas 6.
Peel, core and slice about 5mm thick:

> *1.35kg apples (Cox's Orange Pippin, Granny Smith and*
> *Discovery are good choices)*

Roll out into a 35-cm circle:

> *One 300-g disc of Shortcrust Pastry (p. 90)*

Brush off any excess flour and transfer the dough to a baking sheet lined with baking parchment. Let it firm up in the refrigerator for 10 minutes or so. Take it out of the refrigerator and lay apple slices end to end in a circle around the circumference, leaving a 3.5-cm border. Arrange the remaining apple slices within this circle in tight overlapping concentric circles. The apples should be about 1½ layers thick. Fold the dough border over the apples.
Melt:

> *3 tablespoons butter*

Brush the folded dough border generously with butter and then dot the tops of the apples with the rest. Sprinkle the crust with:

    2 tablespoons sugar

Sprinkle the apples with:

    2 to 3 tablespoons sugar

Bake on the bottom rack of the oven for 45 to 55 minutes, until the crust is golden brown on the bottom. Slide off the pan and cool on a rack.

Custard and Ice Cream

The easily mastered recipes in this chapter are all about the velvety, smoothing properties of eggs and the simple but delicate process of cooking them to a luscious thickness. You will be able to make innumerable egg-based custards, puddings, sweet sauces and ice-cream mixes once you've learned the basic techniques. Making ice creams and custards from scratch gives you the versatility to make whatever unusual flavours you might choose (some of my favourites are honey, caramel and fresh mint), and of course they will be all the better for being made from fresh local organic eggs.

POURING CUSTARD

When gently cooked together in a saucepan, milk, egg yolks and sugar become a simple pouring custard, or crème anglaise. Served on its own, in a chilled cup, crème anglaise can be a delightfully simple dessert, but more often it is a sauce served to complement sliced fresh fruit, baked and poached fruit, and cakes.

Only the yolks of eggs are used to make pouring custard. When slowly heated, the yolks thicken, adding richness and body to the milk. The standard ratio of egg yolks to milk for custard is 2 yolks to 225ml milk. Separate the eggs, saving the whites for another purpose. Put the egg yolks into a small bowl and mix them lightly, just until they are broken up. Too much stirring or whisking will make them foamy. Heat the milk in a heavy-bottomed saucepan with sugar and a split vanilla pod. (Vanilla extract can be used instead of vanilla pod, but the flavour will not be quite the same and the visual effect of the tiny black seeds floating in the custard will be lost.)

The milk is heated to dissolve the sugar, steep the vanilla pod, and thicken the yolks. Heat it just to the point where little bubbles are forming around the sides of the pan and the milk is steaming; do not let it boil. When the milk is hot, the egg yolks are added, but first they are thinned and warmed with a little of the hot milk. Whisk a ladleful of the milk into the yolks and then pour them, stirring all the while, into the hot milk.

Now comes the most important step. If overheated, the egg yolks will scramble and separate from the milk. To avoid this, stir the hot mixture constantly over medium heat. I like to use a wooden spoon with a bowl that has a flat end, almost like a spatula. Stir in a figure-eight pattern, covering the entire bottom of the pan. The bottom of the pan is where the heat is strongest and where overcooking is most likely to happen (this is why it is important to use a heavy-bottomed saucepan). Don't forget to scrape the corners of the pan, where the sides and bottom come together. Cook the custard just until it thickens and coats the back of the spoon. I find this easier to see with a dark-coloured wooden spoon. Run your finger along the length of the back of the spoon. If the mixture stays parted and does not drip back across the line created by your finger, then it is done. The temperature at which this occurs is 170°F. The other visual signal I watch for is when the mixture starts to steam profusely, the way other liquids do just before they are going to boil. Keep checking the custard while you are stirring; it will remain the same for a while and then thicken quickly, almost abruptly, when the proper temperature is reached.

Have a strainer and bowl ready before you start cooking. Once the custard has thickened, immediately remove it from the heat, stir it vigorously for a minute or two and then pour it through the strainer into the bowl. Stir the custard to cool it further and stop it from cooking. Retrieve the vanilla pod from the strainer and squeeze it into the custard. A lot of seeds and flavour will come out. Serve the custard right away or chill, covering tightly once cold. The custard will thicken further as it cools. Stir well before serving.

For variety, pouring custard or crème anglaise can be flavoured with fruit purées, espresso, caramel, chocolate, or liquors such as rum, Cognac or other eaux-de-vie. Flavoured pouring custard becomes ice cream when enriched with cream and frozen in an ice-cream maker. The custard can be made slightly thicker with an extra egg yolk, or enriched by substituting single cream for part or all of the milk.

Custard can also be baked in the oven rather than on the stovetop. An example is *pots de crème*, rich custards made with cream (or a mixture of double cream and single cream or milk), in the same ratio of 2 yolks to 225ml of liquid. Pour the yolk and cream mixture into a heat-proof ceramic baking dish or into little ramekins and bake in a hot-water bath, or *bain-marie*, to protect the custard from the direct heat of the oven. Bake in a pre-heated 180°C/350°F/gas 4 oven until the sides are set but the centre of the custard is still loose and wobbly. Remove the baked custards from the water to cool.

Flan and other custards that can be unmoulded after being baked are made with egg yolks and whole eggs. The egg whites add body and structure to the custard, allowing it to stand up on its own. Classically flan is made with milk, which makes it a lighter custard. The standard ratio for flan is 1 egg yolk and 1 egg to 225ml of milk.

VANILLA POURING CUSTARD
(CRÈME ANGLAISE)
Makes 1 litre

Separate:
> *4 eggs*

Reserve the whites for another purpose. Whisk the yolks just enough to break them up. Pour into a heavy-bottomed saucepan:
> *450ml milk*
>
> *3 tablespoons sugar*

Scrape into the pot the seeds from:
> *A 5-cm piece of vanilla pod, split lengthwise*

Add the vanilla pod. Set a strainer over a heatproof bowl. Heat the milk over medium heat, stirring occasionally to dissolve the sugar. When hot, whisk a little of the milk into the egg yolks and then whisk the yolks into the hot milk. Cook over medium heat, stirring constantly, until the mixture thickens just enough to coat the back of the spoon. Do not let it boil. Remove from the heat and quickly strain. Serve warm or chilled.

FRUIT CURD

Fruit curds, of which lemon curd is a prime example, are a sort of fruit custard, but made without milk or cream. To make lemon curd, a mixture of lemon juice, zest, sugar, eggs and butter is gently cooked until thick. When cooled, the curd is thick enough to spread. Rich and luscious with the bright tang of lemon, lemon curd is a classic topping for toast or scones, but it is much more versatile than that. Baked in a sweet pastry shell it makes an incredible lemon tart, which can be topped with meringue. It can also serve as a filling for cookies, cakes and pastries (I love lemon éclairs), or it can be swirled into just-churned French vanilla ice cream.

Lemons are the classic fruit used to make curd, but they are by no means the only one. Any citrus fruit can be used – limes, oranges, grapefruit, tangerines, and so on – as well as purées of berries such as raspberries or blackberries. Mix the zest and juice (in citrus curds, the zest plays as large a part in the flavour as the juice) or berry purée with sugar and eggs and butter, and cook the mixture the same way as an egg custard: in a heavy-bottomed saucepan, stirring constantly, over medium heat, until it coats the back of a spoon. Take care not to boil the mixture or the eggs will curdle. Pour into a bowl or glass jars to cool. The curd will continue to thicken as it cools. Store, refrigerated, in a tightly sealed container for up to 2 weeks.

LEMON CURD
Makes 450ml

Wash and dry:
  4 lemons
Grate the zest of one of the lemons on the small holes of a grater. Juice the lemons; there should be about 100ml juice.
Beat until just mixed:
  2 eggs
  3 egg yolks
  2 tablespoons milk
  100g sugar
  ¼ teaspoon salt (omit if using salted butter)
Stir in the lemon juice and zest and add:
  75g butter, cut into small pieces
Cook the mixture in a small nonreactive heavy pan, stirring constantly, over medium heat until it is thick enough to coat a spoon. Do not boil or the eggs will curdle. When thick, pour into a bowl or glass jars to cool. Cover and refrigerate.

MAKING ICE CREAM

Ice cream is universally loved – and fresh homemade ice cream is the most desirable of all. There are basically two versions. The first is simply sweetened and flavoured cream, frozen. The second is a frozen custard made with sweetened cream and egg yolks, which produces a richer, smoother ice cream. They both have their charms, although I lean towards the frozen custard kind.

Ice cream can be made with all cream or a mixture of double cream and single cream or milk. Flavours tend to be more pronounced in ice cream when it is lightened with single cream or milk. Heat the cream to dissolve the sugar (or honey). At this point the cream can be infused with other flavourings, such as vanilla pod, coffee beans, herbs or finely chopped toasted nuts. Let the flavourings infuse for about 20 minutes, then strain them out and chill the liquid. Fruit purées and extracts are added after the mixture has cooled. Such solid flavourings as chopped fruit, nuts or grated chocolate are best stirred in after the ice cream has been frozen; added earlier, they impede the freezing process. To make a custard-based ice cream, strain the warm cream, mix with egg yolks and cook until thick. Chill well before freezing.

Ice cream can be frozen in a shallow pan or tray but it will have a much smoother texture if frozen in a machine. The constantly moving paddle, or dasher, breaks up the ice crystals and works a small amount of air into the mix as it freezes. There are a variety of ice-cream machines on the market. The traditional machines consist of a wooden bucket that holds a metal canister, which can be surrounded by crushed ice and rock salt. The salt lowers the freezing temperature of the ice, making the ice cream freeze more quickly. The canister is fitted with a dasher that is operated by a hand crank or an electric motor. For best results, chill the dasher and canister before adding the ice cream. There are a number of smaller machines that consist of a double-walled canister that is filled with a liquid coolant. The canister is placed in the freezer until the coolant is frozen solid. When ready, it is filled with the mix and fitted with its motor, which turns a scraping arm. The double-insulated canisters are a bit more convenient but take a while to freeze. If you have the space, store the canister in the freezer so it is ready to go whenever you need it. The mix should be very cold before it is added or it may thaw out the canister before the mix has had a chance to freeze. Only fill the canisters about two-thirds full: the mix will expand as it freezes. Ice-cream machines will freeze ice cream in about 30 to 35 minutes.

When just frozen, ice cream is still soft enough for you to stir in solid flavourings such as nuts or candied fruit. The small canister machines have a large hole in the lids for just this purpose. Traditional freezers need to be stopped and opened up. Serve the ice cream right away, or chill it for a few hours to harden further. In a traditional machine you can leave the ice cream in its ice-packed canister right in its bucket (add more ice to cover the top), but don't leave it in the insulated canister-type machine, which won't be cold enough to harden the ice cream. Instead, transfer the soft ice cream to a chilled container and put it into the freezer. Pack the ice cream tightly to discourage the formation of any ice crystals. Ice cream will maintain its full flavour for up to a week, but it will lose its sublime texture. When it has frozen quite hard, take the ice cream out of the freezer for a few minutes before serving, for easier scooping.

STRAWBERRY ICE CREAM
Makes 1 litre

In a small bowl whisk briefly, just enough to break up:

   3 egg yolks

Measure into a heavy-bottomed saucepan:

   175ml single cream

   100g sugar

Set a strainer over a heat-proof bowl. Heat the single cream over medium heat, stirring occasionally to dissolve the sugar. When hot, whisk a little of the hot single cream into the egg yolks and then whisk the warmed yolks into the hot mixture. Cook over medium heat, stirring constantly, until the mixture thickens and coats the back of the spoon. Do not let it boil. Remove from the heat and strain quickly. Add:

   175ml double cream

Cover the mixture and chill.

Wash, dry and hull:

   675g strawberries

Mash with a potato masher or purée in a food mill. Stir in:

   50g sugar

Let the strawberries macerate in their own juices, stirring occasionally, until the sugar has melted. Add the berries to the cold cream mixture and flavour with:

   A couple of drops of vanilla extract

   A pinch of salt

Chill thoroughly, and freeze in an ice-cream machine according to the manufacturer's instructions.

Cookies and Cake

Everybody has a birthday, and everybody deserves a home-made birthday cake – or at least a few homemade birthday cookies. And birthdays are only one of the holiday occasions that call out in our imaginations for something baked by loving hands at home. For children, simple home baking provides a wonderful introduction to the kitchen: it teaches basic lessons in organization, measurement, mixing, oven use and cleanup. For many cooks, baking cookies was the spark that ignited a lifelong passion for cooking. Even people who generally shy away from baking (people like me, in other words) need a short lesson in cookies and cake.

MAKING COOKIES

A vast array of cookie recipes spring from one basic formula: butter and sugar are beaten together, eggs are stirred in for moisture and flour is mixed in at the end. The consistency of the resulting cookie dough can range from one firm enough to roll out and cut, to a dough soft enough to drop from a spoon straight on to a baking sheet, to a very wet dough moistened only with egg whites that has to be piped and thinly spread with a knife on to a baking sheet. (A charming cookie called a *langue de chat*, or cat's tongue, is made from this last kind of dough.)

Beating butter and sugar together until fluffy and light-coloured is called creaming. Sugar is added, and the beating continues until the mixture is light and fluffy again. The creaming process aerates the butter: air bubbles are literally forced into the creamed mixture. These air bubbles expand during the baking, making the cookies light and tender. Butter can be creamed by hand or with a mixer. If using a mixer, the butter and sugar can be added at the same time. Mix at medium-high speed for 2 or 3 minutes (if using a stand mixer, use the paddle attachment). Stop the machine once or twice to scrape down the sides to ensure that all the sugar gets incorporated into the butter evenly. At a pinch, cold butter can be used: just put it into the mixing bowl by itself and beat until soft before adding the sugar. The butter has to be soft to cream properly.

Once the butter and sugar are creamed together, add the eggs and mix well. If using a mixer, scrape down the sides of the bowl as needed. It is important that the eggs be at room temperature, too. If they are added cold, the butter will seize up, deflating the air bubbles, and the dough will resist thorough mixing. Add liquid flavourings and sweeteners such as vanilla extract, liquors, treacle and honey along with the eggs.

Flour is the last ingredient to be added. Be sure to measure the flour the same way every time. This will make your baking more consistent. I recommend this method: stir the flour up to fluff it. Use a dry measuring cup, the flat-topped kind that fills to the brim, and either scoop up the flour with it or spoon the flour into it; then draw a spatula or knife across the top of the cup to level the flour. Don't tap the cup or the flour will compact. Add the flour to the butter and eggs and stir it in until just mixed. You want all the flour to be completely mixed in, but too much stirring will activate the gluten in the flour and make the cookies tough. Mix salt, ground spices and baking powder or bicarbonate of soda into the flour before it is added to the cookie dough. Chunky flavourings such as chopped nuts, chocolate or dried fruit should be stirred in gently after the flour has been mixed in.

Dough for drop cookies can be baked right away or chilled and baked later. Cookies that are to be shaped or rolled out often require chilling first to firm up the dough. Many cookie doughs can be rolled into logs, chilled and then sliced into neat cookies to bake. Shape the logs into ovals, squares or rectangles for different shapes. The logs can be frozen for up to 2 months and the sliced cookies require no defrosting before baking. Slice off as many cookies as needed and return the rest to the freezer for later.

To bake cookies properly it is worth investing in one or two heavy baking sheets. They help the cookies to bake evenly, particularly by keeping them from browning too much on the bottom. An oven thermometer is helpful for determining your oven's actual temperature. I like to line baking sheets with baking parchment or a silicone mat, both of which keep cookies from sticking and make cleanup much easier. The baking parchment can be reused from batch to batch.

Bake the cookies in the centre of a preheated oven. Adjust your oven racks if necessary. Every oven has a hot spot where the cookies will bake more quickly. To compensate for this, rotate the baking sheets halfway through the baking. Turn the baking sheets around, both front to back and top to bottom, switching oven racks. If the cookies are browning too quickly on the bottom, slide another baking sheet underneath the hot one to slow it down. Cookies at the edges of a baking sheet may bake more quickly; if so, remove them when they are done and return the rest to the oven to finish. Let the cookies cool completely before storing.

GINGER SNAPS
Makes thirty 5-cm cookies

Preheat the oven to 180°C/350°F/gas 4.
Measure into a bowl and stir together:
>   *200g flour*
>   *1½ teaspoons bicarbonate of soda*
>   *½ teaspoon salt*
>   *2 teaspoons ground cinnamon*
>   *1½ teaspoons ground ginger*

In another bowl, beat until soft and fluffy:
>   *175g butter, softened*

Add:
>   *150g sugar*

Cream the mixture until light and fluffy. Stir in, mixing well:
>   *½ teaspoon vanilla extract*
>   *75ml treacle*
>   *1 egg, at room temperature*

Stir in the dry ingredients. Don't overmix, but make sure they are completely incorporated. Wrap the dough in polythene and chill for 2 hours. On a lightly floured board, roll out the dough 2 to 5mm thick. Cut out the cookies with a floured cutter and place them 3.5cm apart on a baking sheet lined with baking parchment or a silicone mat. Bake until puffed and set, about 10 minutes. Let the cookies cool for 1 to 2 minutes before removing from the pan.

BISCOTTI

In Italian, *biscotti* means 'twice-cooked'. Biscotti are baked first in long loaves, then sliced into thick cookies and baked again until lightly toasted. The cookies are crisp and dry, and store well; and I like the fact that they are not extremely sweet. Various ingredients such as nuts, chocolate, spices, liquor and dried fruits are added for flavour. I make biscotti flavoured with lightly toasted almonds and aniseed. They go equally well with a cup of coffee or tea or a glass of wine.

The biscotti recipe I use most often has no butter. Eggs and sugar are beaten together until they increase in volume, turn light in colour, and form a ribbon when you lift up the whisk or beaters. This means the mixture will fall back on to itself slowly and thickly in a ribbon-like pattern. When the eggs are warm it will take about 3 or 4 minutes to beat the eggs to this point; when they are cold, it can take up to 10 minutes. If you have forgotten to take the eggs out of the refrigerator in advance, warm them for a few minutes in their shells in a bowl of almost-hot water.

Air trapped in the beaten egg mixture lightens the texture of biscotti. Be careful to stir in the flour only until it is just incorporated, and then gently fold in the other ingredients so as not to deflate the eggs. Form the dough into long loaves on a baking sheet lined with baking parchment. The dough will be very wet and sticky. Wet your hands before touching it to keep them from sticking. Use a spoon and your hands to smooth the logs. Bake them until golden and set. When removed from the oven, the loaves are quite delicate until cooled. Carefully pull the whole sheet of parchment with the loaves straight on to a cooling rack. When cool, slice the loaves with a long serrated bread knife (on a diagonal, for longer cookies). Spread the cookies out on the baking sheet and bake again until golden and toasted. They will keep for up to a month in an airtight container.

ANISE–ALMOND BISCOTTI
Makes about 40 cookies

Preheat the oven to 180°C/350°F/gas 4.
Spread out on a baking sheet and toast in the oven for 5 minutes:

150g whole almonds

Let cool and chop coarsely.
Measure and stir together:

300g unbleached plain flour

1 teaspoon baking powder

¾ teaspoon aniseed

In another bowl, combine:

3 eggs, at room temperature

200g sugar

¼ teaspoon grated lemon zest

Beat together until the mixture forms a ribbon. Stir in the flour mixture until just incorporated and then gently fold in the almonds.

On a baking-parchment-lined baking sheet, form the dough into two 7.5-cm-wide loaves, about 7.5cm apart. Smooth the loaves with damp hands. Bake for 25 minutes, or until lightly golden. Remove the loaves from the oven and let cool for about 10 minutes. Lower the oven temperature to 150°C/300°F/gas 2. Cut the cooled loaves into 1-cm-thick cookies and place cut side down on 2 baking sheets. Cook for 10 minutes, turn the cookies over and cook for another 10 minutes, or until golden brown.

MAKING A CAKE

It's a satisfying thing, knowing how to make a classic buttery, delicate cake from scratch. A 1-2-3-4 cake is a version of a traditional recipe the name of which refers to the American-cup quantities of butter, sugar, flour, and eggs – the cake's principal ingredients. The cake has wonderful flavour, and the texture is moist and tender, the two qualities that make a cake great. Unadorned, it makes a simple tea cake perfectly suited for a garnish of fresh fruit; decorated, it can be anything from a birthday cake to a wedding cake to individual cupcakes.

Baking requires more precision than most other types of cooking and it is enormously helpful to gather and measure your ingredients carefully at the outset. The first steps to baking a cake are preparing the pan, preheating the oven and assembling the ingredients. To prepare the cake tin, first butter the inside, spreading softened butter thinly and evenly with a butter wrapper, a brush or your fingers. To ensure that the cake does not stick to the bottom, line it with baking parchment: trace the bottom of the tin on a piece of baking parchment, cut it out and put it into the tin. Butter the piece of baking parchment as well. The recipe may also say to flour the tin. To do so, put a couple of tablespoons of flour (or cocoa, for chocolate cakes) into the tin and carefully rotate it to distribute the flour evenly over the butter. Once all the butter has been coated with flour, invert the tin and tap out all the excess.

Bake cakes in a preheated oven. The first few minutes of baking determine how a cake will rise. When the oven is not up to temperature, the rising is inhibited. Preheat the oven for at least 15 minutes and check the temperature with an oven thermometer before putting the cake in to bake.

Having all your ingredients measured and at room temperature before you start makes the whole process smoother and easier, and you'll be less likely to make mistakes. Room-temperature ingredients are essential. Adding cold ingredients will cause the mixture to 'seize', or shrink and deflate, which will compromise the cake's texture, making it dense instead of light. Butter needs to be soft; take it out of the refrigerator to soften for at least 30 minutes. It will soften faster if you cut it up into small pieces. Measuring out the milk and separating the eggs ahead of time will give them time to warm up.

The flour is mixed with salt and a chemical leavener, either baking powder or bicarbonate of soda. For a lighter, more delicate cake, use self-raising cake flour; it is made from soft wheat, which has a lower protein content, and is milled very fine. Pastry flour is the next-best thing. Plain flour can be used, too, but the texture of the cake will be heavy and coarse; fine cake flour makes a big difference. The most accurate measure of flour is by weight, but most recipes in the United States use measurements in volume. The amount of flour added to a cake makes a big difference in its final texture so, for consistency, try to measure the flour exactly the same way every time. For delicate cakes I suggest sifting more flour than the recipe calls for before you measure it. Sifting aerates the flour and makes it easier to mix, which helps to keep the cake light. Scoop or spoon the flour into the measuring cup (use a dry measuring cup, with a flat rim and no pour spout) and scrape a spatula or knife across the top of the cup to level it. Don't compact the flour by tapping the cup or smashing the flour down. After sifting and measuring, stir the other dry ingredients into the flour. Many recipes instruct you to sift the dry ingredients together, but stirring does a better job of mixing the ingredients.

The first step in assembling the creamed mixture is to cream the softened butter with sugar. Beat the butter and sugar until the mixture is soft and fluffy and very light in colour. If you do this with an electric mixer the butter and sugar can be beaten together from the start, but when beating by hand beat the butter well first before adding the sugar. Creaming the butter and sugar will take 5 to 10 minutes. Don't skimp on this: it is the key to a soft, voluminous, tender cake. The sugar cuts into the butter, creating air pockets, and as the butter gets lighter, the air pockets expand and multiply. This aerated mixture is the foundation of the cake. Room-temperature egg yolks are beaten in one at a time and each is thoroughly incorporated before the next is added. The mixture may start to look a little curdled after all the yolks are added, but don't worry; adding the flour will rectify this in the end.

Next, the flour mixture and room-temperature milk are mixed in alternately, starting and ending with the flour. For best results, use a sifter or a fine-meshed sieve and add the flour mixture to the creamed mixture by thirds. The flour doesn't have to be completely mixed in before the next addition of milk. Mix only until the milk and flour are just incorporated. The milk activates the gluten in the flour and overmixing will develop it, toughening the cake. Whisk the egg whites into stiff but moist peaks. Stir one third of the whites into the creamed mixture to loosen it, then gently fold in the rest. Pour the mixture into the prepared tin; it should be no more than two-thirds full to allow room for the cake to rise.

For best results, bake the cake in the centre of the oven; adjust the racks if necessary. If possible, don't disturb the cake during the first 15 minutes of baking. Opening the oven lowers the heat significantly and the change in temperature could cause the cake to fall. After this initial cooking, the structure of the cake is pretty well set and much more stable. Start testing for doneness when the cake is well risen and golden and is pulling away from the sides of the tin. Poke a wooden toothpick or skewer into the centre of the cake. The cake is done when the toothpick comes out clean with no mixture sticking to it. Let the cake cool before taking it out of the tin.

This 1-2-3-4 cake is very moist and can be made a day ahead. For best results, store it in its tin, tightly covered. Unmould it and decorate it the day you serve it. To unmould the cake slide a knife around the edges of the cake tin. Invert the cake on to a plate. Peel off the lining parchment and invert the cake on to another plate.

1-2-3-4 CAKE
Makes two 22.5-cm round cakes

Preheat the oven to 180°C/350°F/gas 4.

Butter the cake tins and line the bottom of each with baking parchment. Butter the parchment and dust the tins with flour, tapping out the excess. Separate:

4 eggs

Measure:

225ml milk

Sift and then measure:

300g self-raising cake flour

Stir in:

4 teaspoons baking powder

½ teaspoon salt (use ¼ teaspoon if using salted butter)

In another bowl, beat until light and fluffy:

200g butter, softened

Add:

400g sugar

Cream until light and fluffy. Beat in the 4 egg yolks, one at a time, and:

1 teaspoon vanilla extract

When well mixed, add the flour mixture and milk alternately, starting and ending with one third of the flour. Stir just until the flour is incorporated. In another bowl, whisk the egg whites to soft peaks. Stir one third of the egg whites into the mixture, then gently fold in the rest. Pour the mixture into the prepared tins and bake until a toothpick inserted into the centre comes out clean, 30 to 40 minutes.

GREAT  FOOD

THROUGHOUT the history of civilization, food has been livelihood, status symbol, entertainment – and passion. The twenty fine food writers here, reflecting on different cuisines from across the centuries and around the globe, have influenced each other and continue to influence us today, opening the door to the wonders of every kitchen.